"For those who are troubled by the growing use of Christian language to support nationalism and exclusion, Michael Austin has the real Good News. His careful study of Christian faith and American values helps us see our nation and the world in a more constructive, loving way."

—Robin W. Lovin
Southern Methodist University

"Michael Austin's *American Christian Nationalism* is what the ancients would have called an enchiridion: a clear, concise, and incisive handbook for anyone wishing to understand the conflict and rancor about Christian nationalism. Until Austin, no one had matter-of-factly set out the political and theological problems with Christian nationalism while avoiding any hint of a polemical tone. In this, he has succeeded admirably. We need this book."

—Joel Looper
Baylor University

"Christianity loses its bearings when it is made to serve nationalist interests. In this concise and accessible book, Michael W. Austin rightly raises the alarm about the role of the faith in US politics, especially since 2016. American Christians who don't want to go down in history as a cautionary tale will take heed."

—Christopher B. Hays
Fuller Theological Seminary

"Michael W. Austin's *American Christian Nationalism* is not merely another condemnation of Christian nationalism—although it certainly offers compelling biblical, theological, and political argu-

ments to show why Christian nationalists misread Scripture and misunderstand American values. But it also suggests a thoughtful alternative form of faith-based political engagement that is Christ-centered, compassionate, and pluralistic, and that places a primacy on Christian virtues rather than political power. For Christians who are dismayed by the contemporary state of American politics, Austin offers a hopeful vision that draws on the best insights from the prophetic Christian politics of the past and applies them to our pluralistic context today."

—Daniel K. Williams
author of *The Politics of the Cross:*
A Christian Alternative to Partisanship

AMERICAN
CHRISTIAN
NATIONALISM

NEITHER
AMERICAN
NOR CHRISTIAN

MICHAEL W. AUSTIN

WILLIAM B. EERDMANS PUBLISHING COMPANY
GRAND RAPIDS, MICHIGAN

Wm. B. Eerdmans Publishing Co.
4035 Park East Court SE, Grand Rapids, Michigan 49546
www.eerdmans.com

Book design by Lydia Hall

Printed in the United States of America

30 29 28 27 26 25 24   1 2 3 4 5 6 7

ISBN 978-0-8028-8435-0

Library of Congress Cataloging-in-Publication Data

A catalog record for this book is available from the Library of Congress.

Contents

Foreword

During 2011–2013, something very insidious began happening on the campus where my husband and I were working. People began taking sides and elevating political ideals over loving their closest and actual neighbors. What was once a community of those who may have had theological and political disagreements yet were able to get along, became a community of hostility, in an *Us versus Them* contest. My husband and I and many others went from being part of the *Us* to being pariahs, the *Them*.

I did not know it back then, but what I was witnessing in part was a resurgence of white Christian nationalism in tandem with an ultraconservative plan to take back institutions that had supposedly drifted to the left. Seeking a safety net for the poor, immigrant, and elderly; combating racism; and caring for creation—all biblical mandates—along with a belief in egalitarianism, were considered beyond the pale. Those desiring power clandestinely and stealthily overthrew our administrators and replaced them with those now known as Christian nationalists. They sought a utopia but used fear, deceit, and lies in their effort to create it. They did great spiritual, emotional, and economic harm to so many people without any hint of regret or remorse. They did it in their zeal and passion for what they believed to be biblical and institutional purity. What I could not get over was how they used godless means to accomplish what they believed to be God's ends. To this day they continue on their merry way, leaving casualties in their wake.

What transpired then was a foreshadowing and foretaste of what happened on a much wider scale all throughout the United States in the following years. However, this is nothing new within the history of the United States. Xenophobia, nationalism, and isolationism raise their monstrous heads in times of economic, political, and cultural uncertainty. And unfortunately, the white American church has mirrored and mimicked the same attitudes and trends within the broader culture. Christians who oppose such postures and behaviors have routinely been labeled unchristian, unpatriotic, leftists, and Marxists. So here we are again; it is happening in our time, in an era with more technological advance than ever before. Our technology may have advanced, but our national character and the Christlikeness of Christians in the United States have not advanced to the same degree as our technology. We are repeating the sins of our forefathers and foremothers. What are we to do?

Fortunately, Mike Austin uniquely lends his wisdom to the chorus of those warning us about what is happening. As he deftly defines Christian nationalism and enters into conversations with evangelical proponents of Christian nationalism, Austin refuses to dehumanize and demonize Christian nationalists. His writing demonstrates that he has tried to understand where they are coming from, though clearly believing them to be in error. He is kind, not sarcastic or condescending, even while warning that "rather than reaching for a towel to wash the feet of others, Christian nationalism grasps for a sword to force others into line." In this and many other ways, according to Austin, Christian nationalism corrupts characters and leaves proponents less like Jesus. Austin's wise insights are too many to mention here; you have to read this easily digestible book to benefit from them.

However, here is one of the many hitting-it-out-of-the-ballpark observations that Austin makes in this book: "Christian nationalism all too often prioritizes power, prestige, and prosperity over service. Rather than uniting us in working together to help one another, it divides us. It seeks power, not to serve those who are in need, but to serve oneself and those who are enough 'like me' that I feel like serving them." I highly recommend this book for those seeking to better understand Christian nationalism, to those wondering if they are Christian nationalists, and to those seeking to follow Christ more closely while living in the United States. And after you read it, pass it on to someone else who might benefit from it, that they too might have the opportunity to become more like Jesus. If we heed the wisdom in this book, this short and wise exploration of Christian nationalism by Austin, who is both scholarly and pastoral, will function as an antidote to the corruption of Christian nationalism and as a guide to repentance.

Dr. Marlena Graves
author of *The Way Up Is Down* and *Bearing God*

Preface

There is a part of me that did not want to write this book. The main focus of my research and writing is how Christians can develop character, with a special focus on the ways that we can cultivate virtues like compassion, humility, and love. But in 2016, I became concerned about American Christian nationalism. Since then, its influence and the attention given to it have only increased, as has my concern. There are many reasons to be concerned. American Christian nationalism damages our witness for Christ, hinders our growth in the character of Christ, and contradicts the gospel of Christ and his kingdom.

This book is a critical introduction to American Christian nationalism. I explain what it is and then describe several important criticisms of this approach to religion and political activity in the United States. There is now a good deal of very helpful research on this topic, but a lot of this work is aimed at scholars. This book is for the person who might not be sure what Christian nationalism is, for the person who might wonder whether or not they are a Christian nationalist. It is also for the person considering whether or not they should be one. It is also for those who are troubled by what Christian nationalism is doing to family members, friends, fellow church members, and our nation. Because I am an American Christian writing this book to help fellow American Christians address this issue, I often use "we" and "us" to refer to American Christians. For those interested in going deeper into the issues and arguments, the sources found in the bibliography will serve you well.

I am grateful to my wife, Dawn, whose encouragement helped me complete this book. I also would like to express my appreciation to everyone at Eerdmans, including Trevor Thompson, Laurel Draper, Lydia Hall, Jason Pearson, James Ernest, and many others who helped make this book a reality. I am indebted to Blake Cullens, as some of his very detailed work helped me develop my thoughts on certain aspects of Christian nationalism in America. Finally, I am very grateful to Antipas Harris, Van Gayton, and Rob Schenck for their work convening a conference in March 2023 at Harris-Manchester College, Oxford University, on racialized Christian nationalism where I was fortunate to be a participant. It was a rich, challenging, and rewarding time in a beautiful setting rich in tradition and devotion to the life of the mind. It is to them that I dedicate this book.

Defining American Christian Nationalism

On the ceiling of the rotunda in the US Capitol, there is a fresco called *The Apotheosis of Washington*. *Apotheosis* means to deify, or make one into a god. Completed in 1865, the fresco depicts George Washington ascending to the heavens in glory, a rainbow at his feet. On either side of him are two female figures, one representing Liberty and the other Victory or Fame.

At the 1912 convention of Teddy Roosevelt's Progressive Party, members sang to the tune of "Follow, follow, I will follow Jesus," though they replaced "Jesus" with "Roosevelt" as they sang.

The impulse to deify our president (and expand executive power) has long been alive and well. On the day of Donald Trump's arraignment in New York for felonies related to hush money payments, Marjorie Taylor Greene compared him to Nelson Mandela and Jesus: "Trump is joining some of the most incredible people in history being arrested today. Nelson Mandela was arrested, served time in prison. Jesus—Jesus was arrested and murdered by the Roman government."[1]

We are unsurprisingly partisan in all this, however. Our deification of the president, and the boundaries we want around presidential power, depend on which party is in office: "The level of offense taken, the degree to which particular groups resist the deification of the presidency, seems to depend on whether they identify with whichever faction currently holds the White House."[2]

There is a long tradition of anointing political leaders as our saviors across the political spectrum. There is also a tradition of seeing America as somehow special in God's sight, often reflected in the words of our presidents over the past seventy years or so. Kennedy, Johnson, Nixon, Carter, Reagan, Clinton, and Obama all referred to America with the biblical imagery of "a city on a hill" (Matt. 5:14).

Declarations of American exceptionalism, which often include bringing together our national aspirations and our religious faith, are not limited to politicians. Many American Christians use the words of 2 Chronicles 7:14 as a way to pray for the United States: "If my people who are called by my name humble themselves, pray, seek my face, and turn from their wicked ways, then I will hear from heaven and will forgive their sin and heal their land." Yet the passage and the promise are given to Israel, and no other nation. This doesn't mean there is something wrong with praying for the healing of our nation. By all means, we should do this. But we must recognize the differences between God's covenant people, Israel, and the United States of America, as well as the differences between the church and the nation, as we pray and live out our faith in the world.

One way that many have misunderstood the relationship between the church and our nation is through their acceptance of American Christian nationalism. While many think Christian nationalism is relatively new, it influenced ideals that shaped the colonization of the Americas.[3] A doctrine known as the Doctrine of Discovery motivated Christopher Columbus's 1493 commission to return to the Americas to claim land and convert the Indigenous peoples of that land.

This theological doctrine justified European conquest and dominion over Indigenous peoples on the basis that converting Indigenous people ensured their salvation and therefore was ultimately for their benefit. Whatever suffering they endured was worth it because they would experience eternal life after their conversion. If the "barbarous" (as conquering Europeans saw them) nations had to be violently overthrown, so be it. At least they would be converted to faith in Christ. European imperialism and the African slave trade alike were framed as service to the Christian missionary enterprise. Of this history, Lisa Sharon Harper rightly observes that the "European conquest of land and people throughout the Enlightenment period was actually a period of wrestling against God for control and dominion over the planet."[4] In this we see idolatry related to wealth, land, and power. The suffering and death inflicted upon Indigenous peoples, which in various forms continues to this day, are a result of wanting what belongs to God alone. He is Lord of all. We are not. The refusal to accept this has yielded great suffering and evil. It precipitated the idea of Manifest Destiny, the idea that God gave the North American continent to the United States. This led to the slaughter and forced removal of Native Americans from their lands.

While forms of American Christian nationalism have been present throughout our history, a contemporary version is being proclaimed more openly in recent years by more people across political and religious domains. Some contemporary Christian nationalists speak and act from good motives and in good faith, though I will argue they are misguided in important and tragic ways. Others embrace and propagate it to gain or maintain power. And still others are grifters in pursuit of wealth. I'm not interested in attacking particular people. There's too much of that in our increasingly polarized age. I am interested in considering and critiquing ideas, however. In particular, I want to consider the ideas propagated under the banner of American Christian nationalism and explore how they conflict with our best American values and core components of the Christian faith.

One reason for my concern about Christian nationalism in America is that I care deeply about my country and want what is best for it. For many reasons, I am grateful to live in the United States. Some of those reasons are captured by U2's lead singer, Bono, in a 2012 speech at Georgetown University's McDonough School of Business:

> America's an idea, isn't it? I mean, Ireland's a great country, but it's not an idea. Great Britain's a great country, it's not an idea. That's how we see you around the world, as one of the greatest ideas in human history. . . . The idea is that you and me are created equal, and will ensure that an economic recession need not become an equality recession. The idea that life is not meant to be endured but enjoyed. The idea that if we have dignity, if we have justice, then leave it to us, we'll do the rest. This country was the first to claw its way out of darkness and put that on paper. And God love you for it, because these aren't just American ideas anymore. . . . These truths, your truths, they're self-evident in us.[5]

These words resonate with me. There is much to be proud of, and to be thankful for, as an American. I love the ideas in our founding documents. I'm grateful that ideas like human equality; the unalienable rights to life, liberty, and the pursuit of happiness given to us by our Creator; and so many other beautiful, good, and true ideas that are vital for human flourishing were put on paper by our founders. I owe a lot of what is good in my life to those ideas, and to those who have fought to make them a reality.

Yet there are also things about our nation that I would change. We've failed to live up to these high ideals in a variety of ways. From the start, we've not recognized and respected the dignity of all, either in or beyond our borders, including women, children, the poor, Native Americans, and the Africans forced here via the evil of slavery. Injustices, sometimes serious ones, remain. There is much to regret as an American. There is much yet to be redeemed in America. While there is still much work to do, we've also made great progress, preserving the American ideals that are worth sacrificing for, as many have, for the good of the United States and the world. The best American hope based on the best American ideals is that all human beings would enjoy dignity, justice, equality, and liberty. But if our best days are to be ahead of us—I hope they are and believe that they can be—the way forward will not be the way of American Christian nationalism.

This is not merely an ideological issue. Christian nationalist symbols were on display at the US Capitol on January 6, 2021. Republican member of Congress Marjorie Taylor Greene believes that the Republican Party should "be the party of nationalism. . . . We should be Christian nationalists."[6] Along these lines, Congresswoman Lauren Boebert has claimed that "the church is supposed to direct the government."[7] But Christian nationalism isn't just a feature of political violence at the Capitol or of some Republican politicians' platforms. According to 2023 survey data, 10 percent of Americans are Christian nationalism "adherents," which means they overwhelmingly or completely agree with a series of statements aimed at identifying who is a Christian nationalist and to what extent. Another 19 percent are Christian nationalism "sympathizers," which means they agree with the statements, but not as strongly or completely. Over 50 percent of Republicans are either adherents or sympathizers.[8] Christian nationalism is here, and it has a wide influence on how people think about their faith, politics, what America is, and what it means to be an American and a Christian.

I'm convinced that Christians, like everyone else, have a right and at times an obligation to participate in and influence the politics of our nation. But there are good and bad ways to do this. There are ways to do this consistent with our faith and with the rights and values contained within our founding documents. As we'll see, American Christian nationalism contradicts central American ideals. More importantly for Christians, American Christian nationalism is harmful to the church and our life together as followers of Jesus. It is corrosive to our spiritual lives and undermines our witness as ambassadors for Christ. It can lead to a dangerous idolatry that puts our American citizenship above our citizenship in the kingdom of God. It also hinders us from loving our neighbor as ourselves.

In the remainder of this book, I have a few goals. First, I'll explain what American Christian nationalism is. Second, I'll discuss some of the ways it contradicts fundamental American values. Then I'll take a look at how this kind of nationalism is in conflict with fundamental Christian values and virtues. Finally, I offer a vision for how Christians can bring their faith to bear on their citizenship, leading us to serve our neighbors, our nation, and the rest of the world in ways that exemplify the best of our ideals.

American Christian nationalism (hereafter shortened to Christian nationalism) can be difficult to define. One reason for this is that not all who identify as Christian nationalists agree about what it is. The same holds for its critics. In the aftermath of the *Dobbs* decision that overruled *Roe v. Wade* and allowed states to determine laws concerning abortion, some claimed that being pro-life meant you were a Christian nationalist. That's a mistake. One can be pro-life without being a Christian nationalist. I've also seen some apply the label to any Christian who supports a law or public policy for reasons grounded in their faith. That's a mistake. This would mean Martin Luther King Jr. would count as a Christian nationalist. Some equate Christian nationalism with conservatism. That's also a mistake. While Christian nationalism as an ideology exists on the right side of the political spectrum, it is not the same thing as conservatism. Others contrast nationalism with globalism, arguing that the best geopolitical arrangement is one made up of sovereign individual nations, rather than one in which power is concentrated under one world government.[9] Others argue that *Christian nationalism* does not signify anything substantial at all, but it is simply a term some use to exclude politically conservative Christians from influencing public policy. Still others think of it as a term merely for people who are patriotic and love their country.

This can be confusing, causing people to talk past one another on this issue. In our search for clarity, we must be careful about accepting and using idiosyncratic and ultimately inaccurate definitions of Christian nationalism. Consider how Paul Miller responds to those who accept and use such definitions: "I do ask that they use words the way most everyone else uses them. People who call themselves nationalists should be aware of what nationalism means to scholars, what it has meant in history, and what contemporary politicians mean when they use it. The word *nationalism* has a history, a scholarly definition, and a specific political resonance."[10] Miller is a conservative, an evangelical, a veteran, a former military intelligence officer, and a White House staff member for George W. Bush and Barack Obama. His goal is neither to silence political conservatives nor prevent religious conservatives from participating in politics. While some want to redefine *Christian nationalism* in an attempt to somehow redeem it, Miller makes clear that this is a mistake.

We are free to ignore Miller's counsel here. Words matter, however. When we refuse to use words the way most everyone else uses them in these discussions, we not only ignore history, scholarship, and politics but we also obscure good communication. Doing so is a mistake. If we're going to have fruitful discussions about Christian nationalism, we need to have a basic shared understanding of the term, one that is sensitive to its historical, scholarly, and political meanings.

So what is Christian nationalism? To answer this question, I'll draw from the work of both its proponents and its critics. This will help us get a fair and accurate understanding. But not everyone who identifies as a Christian nationalist will necessarily agree to the entirety of the characterization I will give. Nor will every critic. That's important to keep in mind. But the characterization accurately describes enough of the views of enough of its proponents to give us a good starting point for thinking about Christian nationalism in America today.

Christian nationalism in America includes most, and often all, of the following features:

1. American Christian nationalists believe America was founded as a Christian nation.

Advocates of Christian nationalism often allude to America's founding as a Christian nation as they make their case. Some point to the writings of the founders of our nation as evidence for this belief. Others go back further in American history. In their book arguing for Christian nationalism, Andrew Torba and Andrew Isker claim that "the American colonies were not founded as secular, pluralistic nations where there was absolute religious freedom, but as *Christian* nations for *Christian* people governed by *Christians* where they would have freedom to practice the *Christian* religion."[11] This claim about the historical relationship between the Christian religion and American government is the one main feature of Christian nationalism that won't be considered in more detail in this book. Historians have examined these issues in detail, and I refer the reader to their expertise.[12]

2. American Christian nationalists believe the government of the United States should promote a particular kind of Christian culture.

Many Christians want to have a positive influence on American culture via politics, education, journalism, the arts, and entertainment media. Some also want to see the government play a role in such influence at the local, state, and national levels. Christian nationalists go further. They want a form of Christianity to be the official culture of our nation, and they want the government to promote it. Miller gives us a good starting point for thinking about this aspect of Christian nationalism in America:

> Nationalism is the belief that humanity is divisible into mutually distinct, internally coherent cultural groups defined by shared traits like ethnicity, language, religion, or culture; that these groups should each have their own governments; that one of the purposes of government is to promote and protect a nation's cultural identity; and that sovereign nations with strong cultures provide meaning and purpose for human beings. . . . The unique feature of Christian nationalism is that it defines

America as a Christian nation and it wants the government to promote a specific Anglo-Protestant cultural template as the official culture of the country.[13]

Followers of Jesus might be especially concerned about the thought that nations provide meaning and purpose for us, when that is a role better played by God, the vocation he's given us, and our service to Christ and his kingdom. We'll consider these concerns in chapter 3.

Here, Miller's final point is especially relevant. Christian nationalists not only *define* America as a Christian nation, but they want the government to *promote* a version of Christianity as the official culture of the United States. That official culture is often referred to as *Anglo-Protestant culture*. What is this? In America, this includes commitments to individualism, individual rights, the rule of law, the English language, Protestant faith and values, the idea that the government has important responsibilities to fulfill to the governed, and the notion that we are to create a city on a hill, or heaven here on earth.[14] What that city on a hill looks like is informed by these and other aspects of Anglo-Protestant culture.

Many Christian nationalists want the government to promote this culture by both custom and the force of law. The kind of nationalism Stephen Wolfe argues for in his book *The Case for Christian Nationalism* includes the claims that America was founded as a Christian nation, should see itself as a Christian nation, and should act like a Christian nation.[15] He argues that the US government and citizenry should be guided by our Christian identity. This means that social customs should motivate people to abide by the Christian values of the nation. The law, in some cases, should coerce them to do so. And law and custom would work together to guide our behavior. The purpose of all this is to guide and assist the members of the nation in their pursuit of both earthly and spiritual goods.

Not every Christian nationalist agrees with every other Christian nationalist. For instance, some clearly repudiate racial or ethnic prejudice and division, while others accept these aspects of Anglo-Protestant cultural Christianity. Some who repudiate racial or ethnic prejudices in their written work embrace them elsewhere. But to be clear, one can be a Christian nationalist without accepting and advocating racist beliefs. As we'll see, however, many of Christian nationalism's adherents and some of its key proponents accept and advocate such beliefs.

3. *American Christian nationalists believe that American Christians should pursue political and cultural power in order to take dominion over America.*

Advocates of Christian nationalism want Christians to gain political power and then exercise it to promote Christianity. Many Christian nationalists contend that this is part of what it means to fulfill the Great Commission Jesus gave to his disciples in Matthew 28:16–20. For example, Christian nationalist activist Sean Feucht has proclaimed that he wants "the Kingdom to be the government" and "God to be in control of everything." How does the kingdom of God become the government? How does God gain control over everything? Feucht's solution is for "believers to be the ones writing the laws."[16] Wolfe calls for a "Christian prince" to come to power who will bring back a spirit of dominion and a renewal of America as a Christian nation.[17] Torba and Isker want Christians to "reclaim and maintain our townships, school board, and counties. Then our state legislatures. Then the entire nation."[18]

Christian nationalists have a particular kind of Christian in mind who should take dominion in these ways. The goal is that Christians come into power who will advocate for a "biblical worldview" that lines up with particular interpretations of the Bible, those that run along theologically conservative lines and fall to the right end of the political spectrum, sometimes extremely so. I point this out not to criticize conservatism. I hold some theologically and politically conservative views. My point is merely that when Christian nationalists say they want Christians in power, they tend to mean only those Christians who agree with them.

4. American Christian nationalists believe that American Christians should prioritize American interests over the interests of other nations.

The assertion that American interests should come first for American Christians is a feature of Christian nationalism that doesn't show up only in books and at conferences held by Christian nationalists. It also shows up on the national stage. In his inaugural address, President Trump stated, "From this day forward, it's going to only be America first. America first."[19]

Why should we accept this? Why America first? One way that nationalists make their case here is by pointing out that a nation is, in some sense, like a family. We prioritize the interests of our own family, even our extended family, over other people in our community and nation. And there is nothing wrong with this. It seems like this is exactly what a good parent would do. Similarly, the idea is that we ought to prioritize our nation's interests over the interests of other nations. You wouldn't allow your child to go hungry or not get medical care that she needs in order to provide food or medical care to another child in your community. Similarly, a nation should prefer, or be partial to, its own people and its own interests, over the people and interests of other nations.

5. American Christian nationalism fuses the American and Christian identities of its adherents.

Christian nationalism mistakenly combines a religious identity with Americans' national identity. This issue of identity, of who we are, of what unites us, is important to understand. For many, "traditional sources of social connectedness and integration such as class, shared understandings of history, national culture and religion have lost most of their appeal," which causes "a profound crisis of identity."[20] With demographic changes, economic challenges, and the decline of religion as a source of identity, many turn to a hybrid identity that fuses being an American with being a Christian. American Christian nationalism is about what it means to be an American (or at least an American in the fullest sense). It's also about what it means to be a Christian.

Often, Christian nationalists draw on their belief that America was founded as a Christian nation to justify the claim that to be an American in the fullest sense, one must be a Christian. Since they believe our American heritage and history are Christian, it follows for them that true Americans are also Christians. This is troubling enough, but from a Christian perspective what is much more alarming is the equation of being a Christian with being a Christian nationalist. Torba and Isker go so far as to claim that "if you are a Christian, you are axiomatically a Christian Nationalist. . . . If you say you are a Christian and you reject 'Christian nationalism,' you are just a disobedient Christian."[21] As we've already seen, Feucht echoes these sentiments, claiming that being a disciple of Jesus means you want God to be in control of the government, which for him happens when only Christians are writing the laws of our land.

Finally, in her book *The Power Worshippers: Inside the Dangerous Rise of Religious Nationalism*, Katherine Stewart argues that the ultimate goal of the Christian nationalist movement in America is power: "It does not seek to add another voice to America's pluralistic democracy but to replace our foundational democratic principles and institutions with a state grounded on a particular version of Christianity, answering to what some adherents call a 'biblical worldview' that also happens to serve the interests of its plutocratic funders and allied political leaders."[22] I both suspect and fear that she is right. In light of this, we must respond to this movement wherever it surfaces. We must reveal its moral and spiritual bankruptcy in order to protect and promote the common good, at the local, national, and international levels. And we must do this as a way of expressing our faith in Christ, who alone is the ultimate ruler of the nations.

2

American Values and Christian Nationalism

From 1892 to 1954, over twelve million immigrants entered the United States through Ellis Island, where they were greeted by the Statue of Liberty. In 1883, American poet Emma Lazarus wrote "The New Colossus" in order to raise funds for building the pedestal on which Lady Liberty now stands.

> Not like the brazen giant of Greek fame,
> With conquering limbs astride from land to land;
> Here at our sea-washed, sunset gates shall stand
> A mighty woman with a torch, whose flame
> Is the imprisoned lightning, and her name
> Mother of Exiles. From her beacon-hand
> Glows world-wide welcome; her mild eyes command
> The air-bridged harbor that twin cities frame.
>
> "Keep, ancient lands, your storied pomp!" cries she
> With silent lips. "Give me your tired, your poor,
> Your huddled masses yearning to breathe free,
> The wretched refuse of your teeming shore.
> Send these, the homeless, tempest-tost to me,
> I lift my lamp beside the golden door!"

A bronze plaque with these beautifully inspiring words was added to the pedestal in 1903. This statue, and these words, communicate some of the key values we ought to hold dear, as Americans. First, *liberty* is clearly on display here. It is the Statue of Liberty, after all. But we can also see other vital American values in this poem. There is an assumption of basic human *equality*, the conviction that all people have inherent dignity and worth simply because they are human. The poor, the tired, those seen as "wretched refuse" in their homelands, are welcomed here in these words. Finally, while it is not explicit, I believe the American value of *service* is present too. Welcoming immigrants to our nation requires that we serve them, meeting their immediate needs and equipping them to become more self-sufficient as they build a life here for themselves and their families, contributing to their own good as well as the common good. While we haven't lived up to these values in all the ways that we could or should, we have a history of receiving people from around the world into our nation. My hope is that we can live out these and other American ideals more fully in the years to come.

Many are attracted to Christian nationalism because it is seen as supporting vital American values. Yet all too often, this is an illusion. There is certainly genuine support for some American values among Christian nationalists. But there is also, sometimes, only a veneer of support for those values. Underneath, there is all too often a vision of America that is anti-American, a vision that contradicts the best values of our nation.

In order to see why, it is important to know that nationalism is not the same thing as patriotism. George Orwell observes that patriotism is a "devotion to a particular place and a particular way of life, which one believes to be the best in the world but has no desire to force on other people." Nationalism, however, "is inseparable from the desire for power. The abiding purpose of every nationalist is to secure more power and more prestige, not for himself but for the nation."[1] I think Orwell is right about the devotion involved in patriotism, though I don't think a patriot *must* think their nation is the best in the world. The more important point is the way in which a patriotic love of one's country differs from the nationalist's goal for their nation: the nationalist wants power and prestige.

Many contemporary Christian nationalists, on the surface, don't seem to fit Orwell's observation. Many are isolationists, insofar as they claim they don't want to force "our way of life" on citizens of other nations. Live and let live. They don't want America to police the world, seeking to enforce our values in other nations. Instead, they see themselves as protecting a particular understanding of the American way of life from external influences and cultures that would, at least in their minds, undermine it. But if any other nation's interests are in conflict with our own self-perceived American interests, all bets are off. In these situations, "America first" may entail American military might being unleashed against other nations in order to maintain our way of life, especially our relatively high standard of living and flow of consumer goods.

Orwell's points about nationalism also come to the fore in a different way when we consider what American Christian nationalists want life to be like within our borders. They want to force a particular culture not only on all who would come here but on all who are already here. This could mean prison for many, and at least in principle, death for some who would dissent. In that sense, they want more power and prestige within our borders.

Christian nationalism actually contradicts several fundamental American values, values that patriotic Americans celebrate and seek to live out in their everyday lives: liberty, equality, and service.[2]

Liberty

Millions of people came to America, and continue to do so, for liberty. They yearn to breathe free, and they come here to get the liberty that is like oxygen for the human soul. Millions of Americans are proud that liberty is a quintessentially American ideal. But what is liberty?

At a basic level, liberty can be thought of as the freedom to direct our lives and respond to what life brings us, with the best that is in us. This requires a society in which we can discover, develop, and deploy our talents for our own good and for the common good. In such a society, everyone will be able to have their basic needs met, including food, shelter, and basic medical care. They'll also have access to education and job training, so they can discover, develop, and deploy their talents. These are some of the preconditions for genuine liberty. Liberty is about the right to live according to our deepest beliefs and convictions, but it is also about our responsibility to live in a way that allows others to do the same. In this way, the basic rights and freedoms of all are safeguarded.

Nationalism is opposed to the value of liberty in a variety of ways. The liberty of those who don't want to assimilate to the nation's favored culture is often violated by nationalist governments, usually by coercion. Often, this is propped up by religious arguments and sentiments, in an effort to legitimate it. Nationalism is also authoritarian, and nationalist movements are disposed to use violence against dissenters. In fact, nationalism is a form of "*internal imperialism*: the rule by a cultural majority over cultural minorities under the ruler group's predominant language, culture, or religion."[3] What could be more dangerous to liberty than this? This is not live and let live. It is live and force others to live the way I do.

Christian nationalism curtails liberty. As Andrew Whitehead and Samuel Perry explain in *Taking America Back for God*:

> Because the embrace of Christian nationalism fuses national and religious symbols and identities, it is able to legitimate its desires for the country in the will of the Christian God, bringing the transcendent to bear on everyday realities. This serves

to inhibit any chance at compromise. There is no room for disagreement. There is no possibility of alternative viewpoints. Such a stance leads to a devaluation of the democratic process where ideally everyone agrees to play by the same rules. . . . Half-truths, shady practices, and authoritarian measures, if in service to realizing a more "Christian" nation, are deemed necessary to ensure the "right" group stays in power.[4]

This kind of ends-justify-the-means mentality is wrong on many fronts. Christians should be deeply concerned about any kind of political engagement, especially when done in Christ's name, that employs such immoral practices that violate the kingdom value of integrity in word and deed (Matt. 5:37; James 2:12–26, 3:9–12).

My concern here is how this mentality undermines our liberty by its justification of authoritarian practices. Liberty and other basic rights should be secured through a commitment to character and the common good. Resorting to deception, coercive state oppression, and protecting the interests of those in power—as long as they are the right people who say they believe the right things—at the expense of the liberty of others is unacceptable. It conflicts with liberty, one of the highest ideals of our nation.

We saw in chapter 1 that one feature of Christian nationalism is the belief that American Christians should pursue political and cultural power in order to take dominion over America. Many Christian nationalists want to limit the liberty of citizens by allowing only Christians to lead the nation. For example, while they recognize the fact that some non-Christians will support their Christian nationalist movement, Torba and Isker state that "leadership and influential positions must be reserved exclusively for those who call Jesus Christ King."[5] These are the leaders of the movement permitted to take positions of political power at the local, state, and national levels. This violates Article VI of the US Constitution, which states: "The Senators and Representatives . . . , and the Members of the several State Legislatures, and all executive and judicial Officers, both of the United States and of the several States, shall be bound by Oath or Affirmation, to support this Constitution; but no religious Test shall ever be required as a Qualification to any Office or public Trust under the United States."[6]

But it gets worse. Christian nationalists also stake out positions that violate one of the most important liberties we have, one that is protected by the First Amendment to the Constitution: "Congress shall make no law respecting an establishment of religion, or prohibiting the free exercise thereof."[7] For example, Torba and Isker contend that the American colonies were neither secular nor pluralistic, and they seem to agree with the notion that religious freedom was intended only for Christians.[8] Seemingly, they want the same in the America of today.

Next, consider Wolfe's Christian magistrate in his ideal Christian commonwealth. This "Christian prince" would have the power to punish "false teachers, heretics, blasphemers, and idolaters for their external expression of such things." This punishment could include not only banishment or imprisonment but also the death penalty. The worst heretics, those who are most determined and fanatical, could rightly and justly be executed by the state if they are "publicly persistent in their damnable error and actively seek to convince others of this error, to subvert the established church, to denounce its ministers, or to instigate rebellion against magistrates." But it's not only such heretics who would be subject to these punishments; it's also members of non-Christian religions, if they "actively proselytize their non-Christian religion or belief system or actively seek to refute the Christian religion."[9] Under Wolfe's system, people are free to *believe* whatever they want, but when they *express or act on their beliefs*, legal restraint or punishment, including capital punishment, would be justified.

These violations of Article VI and the First Amendment to the US Constitution clearly contradict the fundamental American ideal of liberty, especially the freedoms to seek public office and practice one's religion. These Christian nationalist beliefs should therefore be rejected by all Americans.

Equality

Equality is a fundamental American value, professed from the beginning in the infamous words in our Declaration of Independence: "We hold these truths to be self-evident, that all men are created equal, that they are endowed by their Creator with certain unalienable rights."

Equality in this context is not about equality of talents and abilities, which clearly does not exist. Rather, it is about something deeper. The kind of equality in view here lies beneath the many differences and inequalities that humans possess. The American ideal of equality is an ideal that affirms the basic dignity and inherent worth of every single human being. You may be smarter, more capable, or a member of different race, religion, ethnicity, gender, or sexual orientation, but all your interests count the same as everybody else's. We have the same intrinsic worth as human beings, and our fundamental rights should be respected simply because we are human. Equality is central to this. It includes a fair and consistent application of all the laws of our land. This quintessentially American value "is all about respect, honor, fairness, availability, and hope extended to all."[10]

Equality is one of the central components of justice. Our founders wanted to create a new nation in part because of the injustices they experienced, which the Declaration of Independence lists in detail. Justice is a fundamental American value. Injustice is hard to eradicate, to be sure. But we can help justice increase, if we so choose, by working toward greater equality for all. We can work toward a society in which there is basic fairness, in which the basic rights of all are respected so that all have a better opportunity to flourish. In this sense, equality includes the value of opportunity.

People should have the chance to grow as individuals, to flourish, to pursue their goals and vision of a good, successful, and meaningful life. If we deny access to opportunity for pursuing these things, either through the law, the actions of those in government, or the actions of individual citizens, then we are falling short. Equality demands justice, fairness, opportunity, respect, and hope for a good life for all. The more we make this value a reality, the better off we all are.

In the Christian nationalist vision of America, non-Christians may benefit from the laws enacted by their Christian leaders, but they are denied equal status under those laws. Wolfe allows non-Christians to have "justice, peace, and safety, but they are not entitled to political equality."[11] They may not consent, and may even engage in dissent, when Christians create laws privileging what they see as good for Christians. But Wolfe maintains that the dissent of non-Christians can justly be disregarded.

There are also serious problems with Christian nationalism related to racial and gender equality. Richard Land, president emeritus of Southern Evangelical Seminary, a Southern Baptist institution, has asserted that many people on the Left "pejoratively want to tie Christian nationalism to racism and to prejudice."[12] Some may want to do so, but sadly, regardless of where one falls on the political spectrum, there is no need to merely *want* to tie Christian nationalism to racism and prejudice. Some Christian nationalists do this all by themselves.

Torba and Isker state that "Christianity is not limited to any race, ethnicity, or culture. . . . Therefore, Christian Nationalism cannot be limited to any race, ethnicity, or culture."[13] Later, they add that "We don't care about your race, ethnic background, or your past sins because neither does Jesus. We only care that you wholeheartedly repent and follow him."[14] This sounds good, on the surface. Later, however, they worry about Christians being "demographically replaced."[15] Even if they are focused only on religion here, and not ethnicity or race as they claim, this is still a violation of the value of equality. Would they limit immigration only to those who are professing Christians? Moreover, the stated rejections of any racial or ethnic bias are undermined by the words of these individuals on social media. Torba has claimed on X (formerly Twitter) that "God created different ethnic groups. To preserve them is to preserve God's creation and is therefore an inherent good."[16] This kind of thinking undergirds all sorts of racially unjust ideas. If Torba's assertion is correct, interethnic marriage would be wrong, as it fails to "preserve" God's creation of different ethnic groups. Torba has also reposted the following on Gab, the social media platform he owns and runs: "Few societies have been sicker than the current year west and a large part of that sickness is due to jewish media + technology being used to psychologically and spiritually castrate its citizens."[17] In light of these posts, charges of prejudice are clearly warranted.

Stephen Wolfe's activity on X also reveals racial and religious biases. He tweeted in April of 2023 that "White evangelicals are the lone bulwark against moral insanity in America."[18] This ignores the large numbers of Americans of different races, ethnicities, Christian traditions, other religions, or no religion at all who work hard at building a better America, serving others, and securing liberty and justice for all. Back in 2021, he also posted, "Consider how absurd it is to elevate black men when they far exceed all non-blacks in just about every negative indicator, including in sex crimes. . . . The fact is that if there was serious racial oppression since the civil rights era, they have handled it very poorly. This is obvious if you get past the ideology. There is nothing heroic in it, given the level of violent crime and sexual assault (of underage girls)."[19] The actual data do not support Wolfe's claim. For example, according to the US Department of Justice, the criminals who committed rape or sexual assault in 2018 by race were 55.7 percent white and 22.1 percent Black.[20]

Wolfe has written elsewhere that Black people are agents of anarchy in the United States: "There is more to the story of black criminality, but what is important here is that black Americans, considered as a group, are more willing to conduct certain types of public disorder (violence, petty theft, vandalism, looting, rioting, etc.) when constraints are reduced."[21] What more is there to the story, according to Wolfe? This is an important question, because as stated it provides fodder for those who will argue that there is something inherent in Black Americans that explains this criminality, which is false and is clearly racist. If Wolfe did have an acceptable explanation for this claim about "black criminality," it seems he would give it, in order to make clear that he is not racially prejudiced. But he gives no such explanation.[22] While Wolfe and other Christian nationalists bristle at claims made by critics that they use racist dog whistles, it is hard to see how they can avoid the charge. For those paying close attention, the sound of the evil of racism is loud and clear.

There are also troublesome (to say the least) views of women exemplified by advocates of Christian nationalism. Wolfe asserts that "the pursuit of gender equality will do more harm than good."[23] Torba and Isker want the emasculated Christianity of many Americans to end. They want no more "weak and pathetic emasculated 'Christian' men who embrace submissive feminine energy."[24] For them, this will happen when men take dominion over their homes, including their wives and children, and then continue to take dominion over the rest of society. But should men "take dominion" over their wives? Are men really supposed to rule over their wives? It is difficult to see how this is consistent with the American ideal of equality. In subsequent chapters, we'll see how this is also inconsistent with Christian values and virtues.

Upon examining the actual beliefs and goals of many Christian nationalists, it is clear that they deny the fundamental American value of equality. Only Christians who agree with their vision of Christianity and of America are able to enjoy full equality in their America. For this reason alone, Christian nationalism is un-

American and should be rejected by all who embrace the ideal of equality for every human being.

Service

At our best, we Americans serve our family, friends, neighbors, local communities, and our nation. Every single day in the United States, people give their time, talents, and treasure in service for the good of others. Habitat for Humanity has built new homes or improved the current homes of over thirty-five million people. Close to seven million Americans donate blood each year. In 2022, Americans gave over $499 billion to charity. Many others gave money or goods directly to those in need, and those gifts will never show up on a tax return. When natural disasters like fires, floods, hurricanes, and tornadoes strike, not only do people in local communities help each other, but also Americans from around the nation come to offer a hand when those who live within our borders are in need.

Christian nationalists tend to prioritize the welfare of our nation and its citizens over the welfare of the citizens of other nations. It is true that one key job of the government is to secure the interests and welfare of its citizens. For many Christian nationalists, a nation should prioritize the welfare of its citizens just as a parent prioritizes the interests of his children. We'll examine this in more detail in chapter 4 as a failure of Christian love. While Wolfe asserts that "no individual, family, or nation is duty-bound to welcome strangers to the detriment of the good of those most near and bound [to] it,"[25] the value of service contradicts this claim. When we have the means and opportunity, we should help the children of other families and the citizens of other nations. Service dictates that we should not only welcome the stranger but also help those who are suffering outside our borders. This will at times call for sacrifice. Such sacrifice is at the heart of service.

Tom Morris agrees that the American value of service should extend to others beyond our borders: "The value of service has no boundaries or borders. It starts near and reaches far."[26] Thankfully, American service hasn't been limited to those who live in our nation. Habitat for Humanity is not active only in America; it operates in over seventy countries around the world. The US military has a long history of providing humanitarian assistance and disaster relief in other countries. Since its establishment in 1961, over 240,000 Americans have served in the Peace Corps in 143 countries offering help in education, agriculture, health care, environmental care, and economic development. Millions of American Christians have served in other countries, both short and long term, helping meet the physical, psychological, and spiritual needs of people. I write these words only hours after a major earthquake hit a mountain region of Morocco, killing thousands and wreaking havoc on key parts of the area's infrastructure. As I read about this tragedy on CNN's website, there was a link provided to donate money to help nonprofit organizations on the ground in Morocco working to alleviate the suffering and meet the basic needs of survivors. It is a safe bet that many Americans will answer this call.

Service is simply treating others the way we would want to be treated if we were them. It is not just about the work that religious institutions and other nongovernmental organizations do in communities around the country. Service includes the small everyday tasks we do for those we love in our homes and neighborhoods. Providing meals for the family with a new baby or a parent who is injured or ill. Mowing a neighbor's lawn while they are out of town. Watching children for a single mom who works multiple jobs to make ends meet. Helping a child with their homework. Driving a friend to a doctor's appointment. It all matters. The government has a role to play here too. The government should serve all of us, not just a select few. And as we've seen, service includes helping those beyond our borders, as we are able.

Christian nationalism all too often prioritizes power, prestige, and prosperity over service. Rather than uniting us in working together to help one another, it divides us. It seeks power, not to serve those who are in need but to serve oneself, asking, "Who is enough 'like me' that I feel like serving them?" But this is a diminished kind of service that falls short of the ideal we ought to strive for, both in our nation and around the world.

What other kinds of service can we, as Americans, offer the world? Morris makes an excellent suggestion along these lines:

> The everyday patriot in our land is committed as a matter of principle to the good of the entire international community. . . . The Declaration of Independence, we should remember, says that all men, in the inclusive sense of "human beings," are created equal, not just those who happen to live in our borders. This great claim applies to everyone in Afghanistan, Iran, North Korea, Somalia, Ecuador, El Salvador, and any other little part of the earth where, far too often, great numbers of little children have grown up without the most basic freedom and opportunity to become what they are capable of being. The values of our land can be a beacon in the night for all who aspire to the best that's possible in this life.[27]

While we have many problems of our own, and we cannot solve all of the world's problems, there is no reason to choose between service within our borders or outside of them. Service can be a both-and value, not an either-or one.

We can work to increase the well-being of little children here and abroad. We have enough wealth and resources to do both. America has done great good for little children and their families around the world. As one example, the United States has contributed over $110 billion dollars to fight AIDS. Not only have more than twenty-five million lives been saved by this investment, but many more have received services related to the prevention of and treatment for HIV. This is one example of America at its best. We see a humanitarian crisis of epic proportions, and we invest time, money, and energy in response to the crisis, saving millions of lives. We enable mothers and fathers to continue to live, allowing them to care for and love their children. This gives those children and their children a better chance to grow up, to flourish, and to make their own contributions to the good of their communities and the world. This is but one way that "the values of our land can be a beacon in the night for all who aspire to the best that's possible in this life." America at its best has been, and can be, that beacon.

Christian Values and Christian Nationalism

Dietrich Bonhoeffer, German pastor, theologian, and martyr at the hands of the Nazis, reminds us of a very important point concerning what it is to be a disciple of Jesus Christ. He says that "it is the great mistake of a false Protestant ethic to assume that loving Christ can be the same as loving one's native country. . . . Jesus does not talk that way."[1] I've shown in the previous chapter how Christian nationalism contradicts several important American ideals. These ideals matter, not just because they are American but because they are true. They recognize human dignity and offer justification for and protection of many central human rights. Having these rights respected is important for our flourishing as human beings, both individually and in society.

But the more important issue for those who are followers of Jesus is how Christian nationalism is related to our faith. Torba and Isker claim that "a Christian loves God the Father and therefore he loves his forefathers and his fatherland,"[2] citing Philippians 4:20 in support of this claim. But it is not at all clear that this verse supports this claim. In fact, it is clear that it does not do so. Philippians 4:20 states, "To our God and Father be glory forever and ever. Amen." There is absolutely no connection in this verse with loving our fathers or our nation. The context of the verse has to do with the financial partnership between the Philippian church and Paul for the spread of the gospel. There is no textual reason to conclude from the fact that because we love God we should love our forefathers and our fatherland.

Setting aside the total failure of biblical interpretation here, should we love our fathers and our fatherland? Are there other reasons to do so? We certainly should love all people, including our forefathers. That is the clear example and teaching of Jesus and the authors of the Bible—though the ways we might be able to love them will be fairly limited, since they are all dead. But should we love our fatherland? In one sense, love of country is a good thing. But in another, it is deeply problematic. Love of Jesus and love of country can come into conflict. In fact, since every single nation is made up of fallen humanity and led by fallen human beings, love of Jesus and love of country will inevitably come into conflict.

Christians should reject Christian nationalism, because the demands of discipleship to Jesus conflict with the call of Christian nationalism on our lives. Christian nationalism conflicts with Christian values.

Fleeing from Idolatry

In 1 Corinthians 10:14, Paul urges his readers to "flee from idolatry" (NIV). Yet Christian nationalism, to put it bluntly, is all too often idolatrous. Bonhoeffer faced a German form of idolatrous Christian nationalism that was put into the service of Hitler and the Nazi regime. He saw the German church bow at the altar of nationalism but refused to follow suit. He has much wisdom to offer the American church today. His words, while aimed at others in a very different time and place, are relevant for us. In 1934, Bonhoeffer preached a sermon on 2 Corinthians 12:9, which says, "But he said to me, 'My grace is sufficient for you, for my power is made perfect in weakness.' Therefore I will boast all the more gladly about my weaknesses, so that Christ's power may rest on me." In his sermon, Bonhoeffer makes the following observation: "Christianity has adjusted itself much too easily to the worship of power. It should give much more offense, more shock to the world, than it is doing. Christianity should take a much more definite stand for the weak than to consider the potential moral right of the strong."[3]

While there are certainly differences between the German Christian nationalism of Bonhoeffer's era and the American Christian nationalism of today, there are significant similarities. Both contradict fundamental Christian values. They bow at the altar of power, disregard the needs of the weak, and emphasize the desires of the strong. Christian nationalism leads to the exaltation of the nation over God, of our obligations to our fellow Americans over the broader obligations of Christian ethics. It not only worships power, but at times it worships the nation itself as a god. This is idolatry. This is not the way of Jesus.

Christian nationalism distorts "the faith that was once and for all handed on to the saints" (Jude 3) in various ways. For example, it fails to fully appreciate the significance of the truth that all human beings bear God's image, that we all equally have inherent dignity and worth. This naturally leads to support for various kinds of injustice. Christian nationalism also hinders community with others, including fellowship with other Christians. It can even destroy it. Christian nationalism elevates some of our founding documents, not always to the same level as Scripture, but often way too close for comfort. There is a "We the People Bible" with an upside-down American flag on the cover, representing our alleged national distress. It also includes copies of the Constitution, the Declaration of Independence, the Bill of Rights, and the Pledge of Allegiance, alongside the canon of Scripture. Why would a Christian want such a thing?

More troubling is the advice of Michael Flynn, retired US Army Lt. General and former National Security Adviser in the Trump administration (briefly), who is now actively involved in the spread of Christian nationalism. He's a frequent headliner for the ReAwaken America Tour, which holds large events at churches and other venues around the country. The events include the promotion of both Christian nationalism and a variety of conspiracy theories. At one such event, Flynn said, "A pastor, a priest, they cannot stand there at the pulpit—nowhere else in the world—they cannot stand there at the pulpit and preach the Bible without the United States Constitution," and that because of this, pastors "ought to be up there preaching the Constitution as much or more than the Bible."[4]

This is at best terrible advice, and at worst outright idolatry. The word of God, not the Constitution, "is living and active and sharper than any two-edged sword, piercing until it divides soul from spirit, joints from marrow; it is able to judge the thoughts and intentions of the heart" (Heb. 4:12). Scripture, not the US Constitution, "is God-breathed and is useful for teaching, rebuking, correcting and training in righteousness, so that the servant of God may be thoroughly equipped for every good work" (2 Tim. 3:16–17 NIV).

Contrary to the protests of its proponents, Christian nationalism can become a form of idolatry. Strikingly, some Christians acquiesce to the idolatrous nature of nationalism, accepting the notion that loyalty to one's nation satisfies our desire for transcendence, which is shocking in its acceptance of nationalism's religious nature.[5] Why would a Christian seek transcendence from or give ultimate loyalty to their nation? Doing so is nothing less than idolatry for followers of Jesus, giving the nation a place in our lives that should be reserved for God alone. We cannot accept Christian nationalism and remain faithful to the way of Christ. In this case, there is no middle ground or compromise. And while Torba and Isker explicitly deny charges of idolatry, when your devotion to your nation leads you to ask "Who is my neighbor?" in order to avoid considering the needs and even the rights of others, it is hard to avoid the conclusion that some measure of idolatry is in play.[6]

Unfortunately, there are various examples of people placing their duties to nation over their clear responsibilities to God. When asked why he came to think evangelical Christianity in America is in crisis, Russell Moore shared from his experience:

> It was the result of having multiple pastors tell me, essentially, the same story about quoting the Sermon on the Mount, parenthetically, in their preaching—"turn the other cheek"—to have someone come up after to say, "Where did you get those liberal talking points?" And what was alarming to me is that in most of these scenarios, when the pastor would say, "I'm literally quoting Jesus Christ," the response would not be, "I apologize." The response would be, "Yes, but that doesn't work anymore. That's weak." And when we get to the point where the teachings of Jesus himself are seen as subversive to us, then we're in a crisis.[7]

Indeed, when we've reached this point, we are in a serious crisis. When Christians not only ignore but intentionally disobey the teachings of Jesus because they are thought to be ineffective or weak, something has gone wrong. Let's consider how the dual golden calves of effectiveness and strength function as idols for Christian nationalists.

First, consider effectiveness. If the concern with following the teaching of Jesus to turn the other cheek is that it is ineffective, then we must ask what it is ineffective *for*. We can only judge effectiveness by the goal that is in play. A sharp knife is effective for carving turkey, but it is quite ineffective as a guitar pick. So what are the goals in play for Christian nationalists, for which some of Jesus's teachings aren't effective? As we've seen, the primary goal is political power to use for promoting by social custom and law a certain form of Christianity. The goal is creating an America that is true to their understanding of our founding and history as a Christian nation, and their understanding of the Christian faith.

In one sense, Christian nationalists are correct. Turning the other cheek, humbly putting the interests of others ahead of our own, displaying the fruit of the Spirit including gentleness and kindness, and not reviling in return when others revile us—these are all likely ineffective at achieving political power and cultural dominance. But these are the wrong goals. Our goals are to love God, love our neighbor as ourselves, and manifest the fruit of the Spirit and Christlike character in all dimensions of our daily lives, all in service to Christ and his kingdom. For these goals, such a way of life is highly effective, at least if Jesus and the writers of the Scriptures are to be believed.

What about the idol of strength? Strength in certain forms is of course a good thing. We seek to have a strong faith, to live in a way that reflects a strong witness to the reality of Christ and his work in our lives (1 Cor. 16:13). Many Christian nationalists have a different view of strength, and they end up lamenting the loss of a certain kind of masculinity. We've already discussed how some of them urge men to take dominion over their wives and children. Here, we will focus on the culturally shaped views of masculinity that are often expressed in the writings of Christian nationalists.

Torba and Isker argue that Christian men "must stop being wimps" and that "now is the time for a masculine, patriarchic, crusader, 'Jesus is King' Christian revival." What our nation needs is "to be led by wise Christian warriors . . . who embrace their God-given masculine energy to conquer and lead." They go on to tell us that "the time for emasculated, retreatist, 'tolerant' Christianity is over. We will not tolerate our destruction and persecution in our own countries."[8] Wolfe desires an individualism that rejects the idea of universal dignity and favors warrior virtues.[9]

None of this is consistent with a Christian ethic. Crusades tend toward evil. Patriarchy, past and present, violates the universal dignity that all human beings possess as bearers of God's image.

Jesus tells us that the greatest among us are those who lead by service, not by conquering (Mark 9:33–35). He also tells Peter to put away his sword, because "all who take the sword will die by the sword" (Matt. 26:52). And as for refusing to tolerate persecution, the New Testament provides a clear rebuke. There will be times when Christians not only tolerate persecution but choose to bear up under it for the glory of God: "But he said to me, 'My grace is sufficient for you, for my power is made perfect in weakness.' Therefore I will boast all the more gladly about my weaknesses, so that Christ's power may rest on me. That is why, for Christ's sake, I delight in weaknesses, in insults, in hardships, in persecutions, in difficulties. For when I am weak, then I am strong" (2 Cor. 12:9–10). Strength is not just to be found in fighting; it is also found in enduring suffering for Christ's sake, including the suffering that can come via persecution for one's faith.

In a revealing passage, Wolfe says that

> Christian Nationalism should have a strong and austere aesthetic. I was dismayed when I saw the attendees of a recent PCA [Presbyterian Church in America] General Assembly—men in wrinkled, short-sleeved golf shirts, sitting plump in their seats. We have to do better. Pursue your potential. Lift weights, eat right, and lose the dad bod. We don't all have to become body-builders, but we ought to be men of power and endurance. . . . Sneering at this aesthetic vision, which I fully expect to happen, is pure cope. Grace does not destroy T-levels; grace does not perfect testosterone into estrogen. If our opponents want to be fat, have low testosterone, and chug vegetable oil, let them. It won't be us.[10]

I'm all for good nutrition and physical fitness, but one wonders why all men need to lift weights. And does being a man necessitate this kind of aesthetic? Is the smaller-framed poet who is passionate about God and his kingdom less of a man than the NFL linebacker who wants to use his platform to glorify God and serve his community? Seeking a strong and austere aesthetic and worrying about how much body fat we have seems like a much more culturally informed view of manhood than a biblically formed one. This seems like another aspect of the idolatry of strength, in this case of the physical variety. Men in the Bible aren't commanded to cultivate physical strength. Men, indeed all human beings, are commanded to honor God with their bodies and not be mastered by anything (1 Cor. 6:1-20). We are to exemplify the fruit of the Holy Spirit, which doesn't mention any warrior virtues but does exhort us to pursue love, joy, peace, patience, kindness, goodness, faithfulness, gentleness, and self-control. I can't remember ever hearing or reading a Christian nationalist exhort others to redouble their efforts at growing in kindness or gentleness. This is telling.

We'll discuss the idol of strength a bit more in the next section, as it plays a key role in the misguided views of Christian nationalists who urge Christian men to take dominion of their homes, communities, and nation. For now, it is important to see that they place their misguided understandings of effectiveness and strength above the clear teachings of Christ, and in the name of purported political or national interests. What else is this, if not outright idolatry?

There is another dimension of Christian nationalism that undergirds these idols: the fusing of American and Christian identities. This fusing of identities is a spiritually lethal mistake. The body of Christ is neither dependent on nor beholden to racial, ethnic, or national boundaries. The apostle Paul makes this unequivocally clear. Christians have been baptized into Christ. In light of this, "there is no longer Jew or Greek; there is no longer slave or free; there is no longer male and female, for all of you are one in Christ Jesus" (Gal. 3:28).

Lee Camp makes this very point. He observes that in Revelation (and the rest of the New Testament), not only are those made new in Christ from all nations, but the geographical boundaries of nations are actually irrelevant to them as members of the body of Christ. This was not the case for the Old Testament people of Israel, but it is for the church founded by Jesus in the New Testament. Camp puts the point sharply: "The baptized community is a transboundaried people, holding passports and citizenships only as a matter of pragmatic convenience or necessity, but not as a matter of fundamental identity."[11] Bonhoeffer agrees, and he argues that in the Sermon on the Mount "Jesus releases his community from the political and legal order, from the national form of the people of Israel, and makes it into what it truly is, namely, the community of the faithful that is not bound by political or national ties."[12]

For too long, many American Christians have failed to distinguish their identities as Americans and their identities as Christians. Sometimes, we have unwittingly prioritized our American identity over our Christian one. We have idolized the courage of the soldier and tried to invalidate the courage of the martyr. We have cared more about our investments than immigrants, chanting "America first," rather than joining in fellowship with the suffering. We have preferred what will benefit the United States over what will build the kingdom of God. This is idolatry, and we must repent.

Imitating Christ

According to Torba and Isker, a Christian is "a disciple of Jesus Christ who seeks to take dominion in all areas of life by obeying His commandment in the Great Commission to disciple all nations."[13] In this section, we'll consider such claims about the centrality of taking dominion in the Christian life. In the next, we'll examine Christian nationalist views about the Great Commission.

C. S. Lewis has a different take on what it is to be a Christian, when he claims that "every Christian is to become a little Christ. The whole purpose of becoming a Christian is simply nothing else."[14] So while a Christian is a disciple, the point is not to take dominion but rather to become Christlike, to growing in the virtues of Jesus as we grow in union with him. It is seeking to become like Christ in all of life. As Dallas Willard explains, "As a disciple of Jesus I am with him, by choice and by grace, learning from him how to live in the kingdom of God. . . . I am learning from Jesus to live my life as he would live my life if he were I. . . . I am learning from Jesus how to lead my life, my whole life, my real life."[15] To be sure, Christians in politics should be learning from Jesus how to live in the kingdom of God in their lives too. But they should not use their political power to coerce others in matters of faith that are better left to individual choice. Jesus doesn't coerce us to believe in him, follow him, or serve him. He calls, he commands, he corrects, but he doesn't coerce. This is because he loves us and wants us to become all we can in him. This requires a response of love, and love requires freedom to choose not to love. Because we can trust Jesus to do this in the lives of others as he sees fit, we don't have to try to coerce them to faith or into Christian practice.

Bonhoeffer addresses this very issue. We may want others to come to faith or grow in that faith and experience life in Christ, because we love them. But we are not to coerce them. As he puts it, "I must release others from all my attempts to control, coerce, and dominate them with my love."[16] This is because they belong to Christ, not to me. In their freedom from my attempts at coercion, I recognize and respect their freedom to be Christ's, to be formed by him into his image. When I try to form people into Christ's image, I end up trying to form them into my own image, or my image of Christ's image. Both are mistakes. This reiterates, then, the importance of giving others freedom to come to Christ and be who they are in Christ, rather than seeking to use the government and its powers to intervene in the spiritual lives of its citizens.

We've already seen the propensity of some Christian nationalists to advocate violence as a means of building the nation they want to create, using banishment, imprisonment, or even execution to punish certain people of other faiths. Some call for violent revolution in the name of Christ. Wolfe spends a chapter of his book arguing that Christians can justly engage in violent revolution under conditions of tyranny in order to create a Christian commonwealth for themselves. Violent revolution is justified against the tyrant, defined by Wolfe as "any civil ruler whose actions significantly undermine the conditions in which man achieves his true humanity," which he calls "the complete good."[17] The tyrant orders others to commit evil acts; he governs unjustly, abusing his power in these and other ways. The tyrant "attacks true religion," Wolfe says, and therefore violent revolution against him is justified.[18] Torba and Isker think too many Christians see Jesus as a Mr. Rogers-like figure. They point the reader to the psalms and claim that all 150 of them are "God's war songs."[19]

I'm not an absolute pacifist, but there is a theme running throughout the Bible indicating that God hates violence, and that the kingdom of God is not advanced by the sword. Rather, it is advanced by love, by the fruit of the Holy Spirit, and by human beings depending on God to bring that kingdom to bear on our world through love and sacrifice, not violence. I must also admit that I've never heard anyone claim that all 150 psalms are the war songs of God. They are songs, to be sure, but not war songs. At least not all of them. Some of them advocate violence, and there are different ways to try to make sense of that. But the psalms are songs; they are poetry. They are a record of prayers and songs to God expressing in an authentic way the heart of the psalmist. We shouldn't dash the infants of our enemies on the rocks, though the writer of Psalm 137 speaks approvingly of this. The lesson of this psalm is not that we should do this. Rather, it is that we can tell God what we really feel and think, even at our worst. God knows it anyway. He can handle it. And he will correct us, transforming us into the image of Jesus, if we let him.

Torba and Isker also urge Christians to use violence as a way of exercising dominion: "We must never again tolerate evil and the spirit of antichrist in our culture, governments, education systems, homes, churches, and most importantly in our own hearts." They then instruct their readers, "If you don't have a sword, then sell your cloak and buy one because we have a lot of work to do."[20] First, it isn't at all clear to me how a sword (or any other weapon) will help me deal with the evil that is in my heart. That is a job for the Holy Spirit, and the church, and me. A sword is useless there. Setting that aside, are Christians really supposed to buy a sword and use it (or other weapons) to fight evil in our culture, education systems, and churches? Surely not.

They are referring to a much-misunderstood and misapplied passage from the Gospel of Luke. Given the prevalence of people using this passage to justify violence, let's consider why that is a mistake.

The lessons to be drawn from Luke 22:35–38 have nothing to do with Christians committing acts of violence.[21] The passage does not justify buying weapons for self-defense, and it surely does not justify using weapons to fight a culture war. To see why, let's first take a look at the passage itself, describing an interaction between Jesus and his disciples that is placed right before his arrest in the Garden of Gethsemane:

> He said to them, "When I sent you out without a purse, bag, or sandals, did you lack anything?" They said, "No, not a thing." He said to them, "But now, the one who has a purse must take it, and likewise a bag. And the one who has no sword must sell his cloak and buy one. For I tell you, this scripture must be fulfilled in me, 'And he was counted among the lawless'; and indeed what is written about me is being fulfilled." They said, "Lord, look, here are two swords." He replied, "It is enough."

There are three primary ways of interpreting this passage and then determining the possible implications it has for us today. Some take the instructions of Jesus to buy swords as a justification for having weapons for self-defense. Others see a symbolic warning to the disciples concerning what is to come. Still others interpret it as a fulfillment of prophecy. This last interpretation is the best. Notice that no biblical scholars or theologians argue that we should arm ourselves to fight a culture war.

In the passage, Jesus is speaking to his disciples during the Passover meal. This passage falls within the final section of this gospel, where Luke reveals how the death of Jesus was not the end but a new beginning. The mission of the disciples becomes clear, in light of what God has done in and through Christ. Given the importance of understanding this mission, a proper interpretation and application of this passage is significant.

The first primary way that some interpret this passage is as a justification for arming oneself for the sake of self-defense and defense of others. The disciples will be traveling and vulnerable. In light of this, they should be armed for their own protection. On this view, the point of the passage is that Jesus allowed at least two of the disciples to carry swords for self-defense. When Jesus says "It is enough," the meaning is that two swords are enough for this purpose. No more are needed at present.

A second way of interpreting this passage is by seeing the instructions of Jesus to buy swords as symbolic. The idea is that Jesus was not literally commanding his followers to purchase swords, but rather he was making them aware of the suffering and afflictions to come. In their previous missionary journey, they were instructed to seek out hospitality, taking nothing for their journey (Luke 9:1–6). Now, however, Jesus instructs them to sell their cloak if need be in order to buy a sword. On this view, Jesus is attempting to communicate to the disciples that, like him, they will soon face adversity. The intention is to warn the disciples to be ready for opposition, animosity, and hostility. When Jesus says "It is enough," he expresses exasperation at their lack of understanding and ends the discussion on this topic.

The third primary way of interpreting Luke 22:35–38 is as a fulfillment of prophecy. If we read the passage in a straightforward manner, on its own terms, then we can see that the point of Jesus's instructing his disciples to purchase swords is the fulfillment of a prophecy. After the instruction to buy a sword, Jesus goes on to say, "For I tell you, the scripture must be fulfilled in me, 'And he was counted among the lawless'; and indeed what is written about me is being fulfilled." The prophecy referred to here is from Isaiah 53:12. Jesus is numbered with the transgressors because his disciples are armed, and they are transgressors of the law because of this. Earlier, in Luke 18:31, Jesus has told his disciples that all that the prophets wrote about the Son of Man will be fulfilled. This places the Luke 22 passage within a framework of the fulfillment of prophecy. More specifically, the reference to Isaiah 53:12 comes directly after the command to purchase swords. When Luke reports Jesus saying "For I tell you, this scripture must be fulfilled in me," he is linking the prophecy with the instruction to buy swords. The prophecy is fulfilled by the response of the disciples that they have two swords, which are in their possession when Jesus is arrested in the garden. One will even use a sword later in the Garden of Gethsemane. In Matthew's account, Jesus tells that disciple, "Put your sword back into its place; for all who take the sword will perish by the sword" (Matt. 26:52). This is important here too. Jesus would say the same thing to any Christian nationalist who wants to take up the sword for their cause. At any rate, two swords are "enough" to fulfill this prophecy.

The prophetic interpretation is the best. The point is not that the disciples should purchase a weapon to use for violence against others or for protection of themselves. And it surely is not that we ought to arm ourselves to "take back our country for Christ." Using this passage as a justification for such views is a mistake. Using this passage to justify arming oneself for any purpose, much less to fight some misguided culture war, is to misuse and misapply the words of Jesus.

Christian nationalists often focus on men taking dominion over their wives, over their children, and of course over their nation. A defender of this in marriage might point to passages about wives submitting to their husbands. But all too often when people argue in favor of male dominion or authoritarian leadership in the home, they neglect the context. Before Ephesians 5 tells wives to submit to their husbands, it instructs all to "submit to one another out of reverence for Christ" (Eph. 5:21). Regardless of one's views regarding what the Bible has to say about gender roles, too many ignore the mutuality of submission that is central to this passage. That silence speaks volumes about what is going on here, as does men having dominion over *their* children, *their* wives, and *their* nation.

Whether they discuss leadership in the home, in schools, or in government, Christian nationalists often evince a basic misunderstanding of the nature of leadership as taught by Jesus. In the Gospel of Mark, James and John ask Jesus if he will let them sit at his side when the kingdom comes. The remaining disciples are upset when they find out about this request for honor. In reply, Jesus corrects them all:

> You know that those who are regarded as rulers of the Gentiles lord it over them, and their high officials exercise authority over them. Not so with you. Instead, whoever wants to become great among you must be your servant, and whoever wants to be first must be slave of all. For even the Son of Man did not come to be served, but to serve, and to give his life as a ransom for many. (Mark 10:42–45)

I haven't read every single thing written by Christian nationalists in print and online, but I have read a good deal. I haven't seen this passage discussed by a Christian nationalist, ever. For Jesus, leaders aren't to exercise dominion—they aren't focused on conquering. They don't grasp for power in order to lord it over others, punishing those they see as heretics, even to the point of death. Instead, they serve. They sacrifice. They love.

Dominion, as first set out in the book of Genesis, is not about domination or control. Others have interpreted dominion in these ways and have used their interpretation to justify all sorts of environmental destruction and abuse. Dominion is better thought of as stewardship. Adam and Eve are told to care for creation, not dominate or control it. Stewards care for something that belongs to another. The earth and everything in it belong to God, not us. He is above all powers, principalities, and authorities, both spiritual and political. Not us. We serve him by serving others, and by caring for all that he has entrusted to us.

There are other problems with the dominion mindset exemplified by Christian nationalists. For example, where do Jesus and any of the New Testament writers talk about dominion or conquering in the context of politics? Where are men called to lead and conquer their nation and the nations of the world for Christ? We are to conquer evil in the sense of overcoming evil with good, but this is done by exercising our spiritual gifts in the body of Christ, not by putting our enemies to the sword (Rom. 12). We have been freed from the dominion of sin, but not for the sake of taking control of the state (Rom. 6:14). Jesus has dominion over all of creation, not us (Eph. 1:19–23). Rather than seeking to exercise dominion, we ought to focus on the way of Jesus, the way of humility, service, and love. Our battle is not against flesh and blood, as Paul writes to the church at Ephesus. Christian nationalists need to take this fact to heart much more than they do, as do we all.

Making Disciples

The Great Commission given in Matthew 28:18–20 is a passage often used by Christian nationalists to support their views.[22] "And Jesus came and said to them, 'All authority in heaven and earth has been given to me. Therefore go and make disciples of all nations, baptizing them in the name of the Father and of the Son and of the Holy

Spirit and teaching them to obey everything that I have commanded you. And remember, I am with you always, to the end of the age.'"

Christian nationalists claim that part of our mandate, given here by Jesus, is to disciple all nations. On the surface, this claim seems fine. But when the idea is applied within their vision of America and the church, the problems become clear. For example, Article XIII in *The Statement on Christian Nationalism and the Gospel* says this about the Great Commission:

> WE AFFIRM that Christ's commissioning of His Church to make disciples of all nations, baptizing them, and teaching them to obey all that He has commanded includes civil authorities who are to be called to repentance, faith, and obedience to Christ. We affirm that the Church is to instruct civil authorities regarding their identity and duties as servants before the throne of Christ. We affirm that this duty is a Great Commission issue.
>
> WE DENY that there is any sphere of life in which the command "teach them to obey all that I have commanded" does not apply, including politics and government.[23]

Likewise, Torba and Isker assert that because of the Great Commission, all Christians are Christian nationalists. They claim that "since America is a nation, America needs to be baptized and discipled into obeying Jesus. The Great Commission means that if you are a Christian you are axiomatically a Christian Nationalist. If you say you are a Christian and you reject 'Christian Nationalism,' you are just a disobedient Christian. To be part of Christ's Kingdom is to bring the kingdoms of this world into submission to Christ's Kingship."[24]

On the surface, this seems like an important role for the church to play, to give those who are working in politics and government the opportunity to place their faith in Christ and be his disciples. And it is. Certainly, the church should also prophetically speak to those in power, challenging and working for change as needed. In his famous sermon "A Knock at Midnight," Martin Luther King Jr. offers vital wisdom when he says "The church must be reminded that it is not the master or the servant of the state, but rather the conscience of the state."[25]

The notion of the church acting as the conscience of the state is important. This is a valid role for the church to play. But this is not what Christian nationalists want, or at least it is not all that they want. They don't just want the church to act as the conscience of the state. If that were all they meant by calling civil authorities to repentance and instructing them about their duties, there wouldn't be a problem. But they want the government itself to be an agent of discipleship for the church. They want the church to be the master of the state. Often, their view is that only Christians should have positions of power in the government, as we've seen. None of this is part of the mandate of the Great Commission Jesus gave his disciples and his church.

The point of the language in the Great Commission about making disciples of all nations is not that the disciples of Jesus should create theocracies, or Christian-controlled or Christian-only governments. That much is clear not only from Scripture but also from how his early followers proceeded in the book of Acts and the rest of the New Testament to carry out this mission. The mission of the church is to reach all nations. The mission of Jesus and his followers is now extended to all peoples, including Israel but now also the gentiles throughout the world.[26] Crucially, "nations" refers to all the peoples of the world, rather than our more contemporary notion of the nation-state.[27] The Great Commission is about making disciples, teaching, and baptizing. This cannot be done *to* nation-states, only to the people within them. It should not be done *through* nation-states, either. The point of the Great Commission is not that Christians should take dominion over every nation-state and use that power to coercively disciple the people who live there. Rather, it is that the disciples of Jesus are to take the good news of the kingdom to everyone, to all people groups.

Jesus has all authority over the kingdoms and nations of the world. We serve him, we serve one another in the body of Christ, and we serve the world, exemplifying faith, hope, love, and the fruit of the Spirit as we go.

The church is to take the gospel of the kingdom to the world, not become a master of the kingdoms of the world. Paul and the other apostles set up house churches; they didn't take over governments. Christ's first disciples and the early church did not try to turn nations into Christian nations by taking over the government and using the force of law. Instead, they shared the gospel, planted churches, and cared for each other and the poor. They loved God and their neighbors. We don't disciple the nations by trying to take over the nations. We make disciples by embodying the kingdom of God wherever we are: home, school, work, community, and church. The church is the agent of discipleship, not the state. Disciples must be growing in loving their neighbors as themselves. This means they don't use the government to disciple others. That is not the role of the government. It is the role of the church, and if we are to love our neighbors as ourselves, such coercion is wrong.

If we are actually going to fulfill the Great Commission, we need to be more like Christ. Unfortunately, Christian nationalism is damaging the witness of the church. Consider the following data concerning Christian nationalists in the United States.[28] A 2023 study showed that, compared to other Americans, Christian nationalists are:

- significantly more likely to believe that "discrimination against white Americans has become as big a problem as discrimination against Black Americans and other minorities";[29]
- significantly more likely to believe that "immigrants are invading our country and replacing our cultural and ethnic background";[30]
- more likely to believe that "Jewish people hold too many positions of power";[31]

- more likely to use violence as a way of handling disagreement in their personal lives;
- more likely, some significantly so, to agree that "because things have gotten so far off track, true American patriots may have to resort to violence in order to save our country";[32]
- more likely to embrace the main tenets of QAnon conspiracy theories.

All of this damages our witness and undermines our faithfulness to Jesus. The first three prevalent beliefs all have racist elements, to varying degrees. No disciple of Jesus should accept any belief that is racist. It violates the dignity all human beings have as creatures made in God's image. I suspect most readers would agree. However, we all have our blind spots, and I think many who believe discrimination against white people is just as big a problem as discrimination against Black people in America either don't know the data, or are ignoring it. There are racial disparities, best explained by past and present discrimination, not only in wealth and economic security but also in education, health, housing, employment, mobility, and incarceration rates. It is simply false that discrimination against white Americans is as big a problem as discrimination against Black people and other minorities in our nation.[33]

Stereotypical and prejudiced concerns about the wealth, power, and influence of Jewish people have a long and awful history. We surely must fight against anything that could lead to repeating the horrible acts of the past against Jewish persons, but also anything that fosters anti-Semitism. Immigration is a large and serious problem, one that our politicians refuse to comprehensively address. But as Christians, the answer is not to talk about immigrant "invaders" of our country who are "replacing our cultural and ethnic background." Some come to our country with nefarious intentions. But is it right to talk of the individuals and families fleeing violence, grinding poverty, or persecution in their homeland as invaders? Surely not. These are people to love and serve. They are not invaders—they are our neighbors. They are the kind of people whom Jesus teaches Christians to help. We have the chance to be the good Samaritan. Will we take it? We should, as we have the necessary resources and are given the opportunity.

We've already discussed violence as it relates to taking dominion, but it is important to point out that Christians are called by Jesus to be peacemakers—"Blessed are the peacemakers, for they will be called children of God" (Matt. 5:9). We are called to love not only our family, friends, and fellow citizens but even our enemies (Matt. 5:44). Peace is a fruit of the Spirit (Gal. 5:22-23). The context reveals that the focus is not inner peace, or at least not merely that. It is primarily about peace between persons, and it is contrasted with "enmities, strife, jealousy, anger, quarrels, dissensions, factions" (Gal. 5:20). The kingdom of God is a kingdom of peace (Rom. 14:17), and as followers of the Prince of Peace we are told, "If it is possible, so far as it depends on you, live peaceably with all" (Rom. 12:18). Followers of Jesus and his way should not resort to violence as a way of handling disagreement in our everyday lives, nor should we be thinking about resorting to violence to save our nation. If we want to save our nation, the way to do it is by loving God, loving our neighbors, serving our communities, voting in ways that strengthen democracy and the rule of law, and contributing to the common good in ways that strengthen our ties to one another as Christians and as Americans.

Why is the tendency to embrace QAnon and similar conspiracy theories an issue of discipleship and fulfilling the Great Commission?[34] First, Christians are to be lovers of the truth and seekers of wisdom in Christ. Conspiracy theories are often demonstrably false. Truth is serious, and as a follower of Jesus, each of us must take care to avoid gullibility, foolishness, and falsehood.

Second, belief in these theories also damages unity in the body of Christ, as well as in society more generally. It prevents good civil discourse and fosters division, fear, and even hatred. An important question to ask is whether the conspiracy theories we are drawn to believe reinforce our preexisting political beliefs. If so, that's a sign that something is wrong. We may be more concerned about protecting our beliefs than changing them when the evidence warrants it.

Third, belief in demonstrably false conspiracy theories damages our witness and hinders our obedience to the Great Commission. Imagine a Christian who also believes several QAnon conspiracy claims, whose neighbor is an agnostic or atheist. They share their QAnon beliefs with their neighbor, undermining their credibility with that neighbor. When this Christian then shares the gospel, including the belief that Jesus rose from the dead, the neighbor rejects it in part because he doesn't think this Christian is credible. Who can blame him? When someone tells you that there is a cabal of Satan-worshiping pedophiles made up of politicians (mostly Democrats), journalists, and Hollywood celebrities, or that the COVID vaccines magnetize the human body, this casts serious doubt on their credibility. Those who want to fulfill their mission as ambassadors for Christ must take special care to be credible witnesses to truth, all truth, in order to maintain their credibility. Is God at the mercy of our credibility? No. God and the good news of his kingdom are powerful. But we have been given a role to play in reaching the world and making disciples, and we ought to be faithful in that role as we share the good news of God's love, forgiveness, and grace with others.

How can we become the kind of people who are credible witnesses?[35] There is a lot to say here. In addition to being careful seekers and lovers of the truth, we must be intentional about our discipleship to Christ. A central part of that is the cultivation of character. We cannot just make ourselves be people of good character, but we do have a role to play as we pursue this goal, in dependence upon God. Several places in Scripture make this clear, but perhaps nowhere is this more explicit than 2 Peter 1, where we are told that God wants us to "become participants of the divine nature" (v. 4). What do we do to pursue this goal? The author of 2 Peter goes on to tell us, stating, "You must make every effort to support your faith with excellence, and excellence with knowledge, and knowledge with self-control, and self-control with endurance, and endurance with godliness, and godliness with mutual affection, and mutual affection with love" (vv. 5–7). It is not grace or effort, but rather grace and effort. Or better yet, effort fueled by grace achieving results that can only be explained by grace. Over time, as we practice the spiritual disciplines that are most helpful to us personally, we will see growth. Fasting, for example, can help us grow in self-control. Silence and solitude can help us grow in faith, in entrusting ourselves to God. These are not works to gain favor with God. Rather, they are ways we can open ourselves up to a deeper and more transformative relationship with Christ. We make more of our selves and more areas of our lives available to the powerful grace of God via the spiritual disciplines practiced by Jesus, his disciples, and many others who have followed him throughout the centuries. This is the way of discipleship to Christ.

Disciples are those who are learning to be like Jesus, to live their lives as he would if he were in their shoes. And this is to "happen within the special and unfailing community he has established on earth."[36] That community is the body of Christ, his church. Kingdoms fall. Empires end. Nations fail. When Jesus said that "the gates of Hades will not overcome it" (Matt. 16:18), he was referring to the church, not the United States or any other nation. Discipleship happens in and through the church, not the government.

Christian Virtues and Christian Nationalism

Character matters for Christians. It is one of the primary ways we see the sanctifying power of God in our lives. It should be one of the primary goals of our lives, cultivating virtue in union with Christ and dependence upon the Holy Spirit. This enables us to become participants in the divine nature (2 Pet. 1:3–11). Yet believing and acting upon many of the ideas of Christian nationalism corrupts our character, hindering our union with God. Nationalism undermines and even contradicts central Christian virtues, including humility, love, and faith, the virtues we'll focus on in this chapter.

One contemporary advocate of nationalism argues that it is conducive to cultivating virtues, in particular the virtue of humility.[1] How might this work? The argument is that nationalism is conducive to humility because the individual holds that (i) the traditions of one's nation possess truth and beauty, and loyalty to those traditions is also true and beautiful; (ii) there is also truth and beauty in the traditions of other nations. This gives the nationalist reason to explore those other nations and their traditions, even making use of them to correct or improve one's own traditions, as needed. This is plausible, at least in theory. We should keep much of the variety of traditions and ways of life around the world alive, and seek to learn from them.

The problem is that there is not a lot of appreciation for other cultures and their traditions among Christian nationalists. We tend to see a lot more American exceptionalism than allowing the traditions of other nations to correct our excesses and deficiencies. We see pride exemplified in warnings about people in other nations and our own who hold "alien worldviews," ascribe to "demonic religion," or are trying to spread "the evil Marxist ideology of critical race theory." We see skepticism and suspicion of other ways of life, rather than respect and appreciation for goodness, truth, and beauty, wherever they are found. Sadly, we also see callousness toward the suffering of others, rather than compassion.

This is not virtue. This is vice. This is not the way of Christ. Christians should follow another path. We should go the way of character, the way of faith, humility, and love. In this chapter, we'll consider how these virtues stand against the values of Christian nationalism, giving us more reasons to reject it.

Faith

Why don't we follow Christ in his way of humility and love? One reason, I suspect, is we lack the faith required to do so. We fear if we give away more of our time, talents, or money, we'll be left somehow vulnerable. We are anxious about putting others before ourselves because we fear our needs won't be met. But we must trust God to care for us, as we step out in faith to care for others. We all struggle, at different times and in different ways, with having faith in God. Trials can test our faith, tragedy can challenge it, and circumstances can strain it. It seems as if some of the impetus behind the embrace of Christian nationalism is fear of change and of the future, rather than a robust faith in God, his enduring goodness to us, and his gracious love for us.

This is a particular temptation for some Christians in America, who have had a good deal of cultural, political, and social power over large parts of our nation's history. Because of the privileged place some forms of Christianity have had and continue to have in the United States, our Constitutional principles of freedom of conscience and religion, our material wealth, and our military security, the temptation to trust in our country rather than Christ is powerful. Do we trust in Jesus, or in the United States? We need to engage in some serious self-examination about this question, whatever we think of Christian nationalism. But a weakness of Christian nationalism is, oddly enough, that it puts its faith in the nation, including the government (once Christians control it), rather than in Christ and his kingdom.

As a virtue, faith can be thought of as a disposition to entrust ourselves to God.[2] This plays out in many different ways across the domains of our lives. At a fundamental level, it means we trust that God loves us and wills what is good for us. It includes belief not only in God's goodness but also in God's power to bring that goodness about in and through our lives.

Cultivating and exemplifying good Christian character is a central way our faith gets put into practice, a central way that faith works itself out through love (Gal. 5:6). Bonhoeffer connects faith to humility and love when he observes that at the core of his being, Jesus "is there for others," and that "faith is participating in this being of Jesus."[3] The church, in faith, should follow suit:

> The church is church only when it is there for others. . . . The church must participate in the worldly tasks of life in the community—not dominating but helping and serving. It must tell people in every calling what a life with Christ is, what it means "to be there for others." In particular, *our* church will have to confront the vices of hubris, the worship of power, envy, and illusionism as the roots of all evil. It will have to speak of moder-

ation, authenticity, trust, faithfulness, steadfastness, patience, discipline, humility, modesty, contentment.[4]

Bonhoeffer goes on to argue that the power of the church is not in the words it speaks but in the human example it offers in the character of Christians. The church exists for others, and not just others in our own family, church, community, or nation, as Christian nationalists prefer. The church exists for everyone on the planet, because everyone on the planet is an image-bearer of God who is loved by Christ. We can't literally love everyone, because we don't have the opportunity to do so, apart from prayer for everyone on the planet. But we have the opportunity to love people in our daily lives, not just in our family, church, community, and nation, but others around the world as well, in numerous ways. Living in deep union with one another and with Christ, exemplifying virtues like faith, love, and humility, enables us to exist for others just as Jesus does. This transformational union turns our hearts and minds away from ourselves, toward the people in the world we are here to serve. It enables us to fulfill our calling as ambassadors for Christ both in our nation and beyond.

This is the crux of the issue, and it reveals an important failure of Christian nationalism. It too often does not include a faith that is genuinely *for others*. Christian nationalism features isolationism, protectionism, and a lack of concern for the *common* good. There is concern for the good of those within the Christian nationalist camp, but less so for those outside of it. Some Christian nationalists want to build a parallel Christian society with systems and institutions that are grounded in their own "biblical worldview." They want to withdraw from society while they wait for the current system to collapse. When it collapses, "the Godly infrastructure we have built will fill the vacuum."[5]

Rather than reaching for a towel to wash the feet of others, Christian nationalism grasps for a sword to force others into line.

Rather than a way of leadership and life characterized by sacrifice and service, it seeks power in order to lord it over others. Rather than loving people right now, regardless of who they are and where they are from, it limits who we consider to be our neighbor. Rather than working to bring the redemptive love, mercy, grace, and justice of Christ and his kingdom to bear on the world, it exits the system until it collapses. Then, Christian nationalism steps in to acquire the power it has been waiting to get.

This is not the way of Christ or his kingdom. God is at work to redeem all of creation, to make all things new (Rom. 8:19–22; Rev. 21:5). But how does God do this? God is not, as many seem to want, like Saruman in Tolkien's *Lord of the Rings*, a leader who builds a vast army to bring all the peoples of Middle Earth under forced subjection to his master, Sauron. God's kingdom has a lot more in common with the hobbits of Middle Earth. Small, humble, but brave creatures who are good, and do good. Imperfect creatures, to be sure, but nevertheless good. And creatures who are willing to sacrifice for the good of others, even to the point of death.

We must have faith that God will make all things new and is at work doing this right now. We must also have faith that God's way of making all things new is best. Faith in what God wants to do, and how God wants to do it, is vital. The psalmist writes, "Do not put your trust in princes, in human beings who cannot save" (Ps. 146:3 NIV), and "Some trust in chariots and some in horses, but we trust in the name of the Lord our God" (Ps. 20:7 NIV). Christian nationalists talk of a "Christian prince" needed to lead us, as if this is an ideal or even a requirement for God's kingdom to come. Many American Christians, including Christian nationalists, are used to trusting in our modern horses and chariots, the might of the US military. But the kingdom of God is not like this. It wields its influence through love, joy, peace, patience, kindness, goodness, faithfulness, gentleness, and self-control, not missiles, tanks, and a disdain for people from other nations and their worldviews.

Rather than waiting for the system to fail, Christians should bring healing and hope to it and the people it harms. Instead of building a parallel Christian society, let's bring redemption to the one God has placed us in now. And let's follow the example of the hobbits, rather than that of Saruman. It takes faith to do this, but we are called to such a faith.

Humility

The humility of Jesus shines brightly when he washes the feet of his disciples (John 13:1–20), setting an example to be followed in our everyday lives. The humility of Jesus was on display as he put others before himself and became the servant of all, even to the point of death on a cross. In humility, we value the interests of others more than our own, just as Jesus did for us. This contradicts nationalism, at its core. Christian nationalism all too often exemplifies the vice of pride, rather than the virtue of humility. It privileges the rights and interests of some over the rights and interests of others, using the power of the state to do so. Nationalism usurps humility's rightful place in a Christ-follower's life. Instead, nationalism encourages the formation of pride in Christians who accept it. Nationalism corrupts Christian character and spirituality. It has a place for humility, but only a gutted form of it.

We can be proud of our nation, in one sense, for the good it has done and continues to do. We can be proud of our best ideals. But nationalism goes beyond this. It can lead to a vicious pride that sees one's nation as the best in the world or the most important in the world, and its citizens as more important than others:

> Christian Nationalism is loving your neighbor. Who is our neighbor? Our fellow citizens and specially our brothers and sisters in Christ. Loving them means protecting them from foreign interests, alien worldviews, and hostile invaders. Christian

Nationalism means placing the interests of your neighbor and your home above the interests of foreigners in foreign nations. This does not mean we neglect foreign nations or do not extend love to them, but rather that we place the interests and world-view of our home above foreign ones. 1 Timothy 5:8 tells us that "if anyone does not provide for his own, and specially those of his own house, he hath denied the faith, and is worse than an unbeliever." Nationalism is about taking care of our neighbors, our families, and our fellow citizens, lest we deny the faith and be worse than an unbeliever.[6]

Following Christian nationalism leads to failures of both humility and love. There are times when any human being, including Christians—perhaps especially Christians, given the example set for us by Christ—should put the interests of those who are not members of our family, our neighborhood, or our nation above our own, due to the nature of humility and the nature of love. We'll consider humility in this section, and love in the next.

The humility exemplified by Jesus and described by Paul in Philippians 2:1–11 is challenging. It also gives us reasons to reject the claims of Christian nationalists about how we should relate to people who are not our neighbors and fellow citizens, including those who don't share our worldview:

> If then there is any encouragement in Christ, any consolation from love, any sharing in the Spirit, any compassion and sympathy, make my joy complete: be of the same mind, having the same love, being in full accord and of one mind. Do nothing from selfish ambition or conceit, but in humility regard others as better than yourselves. Let each of you look not to your own interests, but to the interests of others. Let the same mind be in you that was in Christ Jesus, who, though he was in the form of God, did not regard equality with God as something to be exploited, but emptied himself, taking the form of a slave, being

born in human likeness. And being found in human form, he humbled himself and became obedient to the point of death— even death on a cross. Therefore God also highly exalted him and gave him the name that is above every name, so that at the name of Jesus every knee should bend, in heaven and on earth and under the earth, and every tongue confess that Jesus Christ is Lord, to the glory of God the Father. (Phil. 2:1–11)

Humility is a vital part of being a Christian. Understood in the overall context of Philippians, the humility of Christ and its relevance for us become clearer. Humility has to do with our attitude toward both ourselves and others. What does it mean to "regard others as better than yourselves"? It means that we are to put their interests ahead of our own, because this is what Christ has done for us. In the Roman culture at Philippi, where honor was highly prized, these attitudes and actions would have been highly unusual and quite countercultural. They remain so today. Pride is still a problem for human beings.

We are to look to the interests of others, to put their interests above our own by seeing those interests as more important than our own. This is a key aspect of Christian humility. But Christian nationalists want to limit the scope of humility to our neighbors and fellow citizens, especially those who are Christians. We do have special obligations of love to our fellow Christians, as members of the community of Christ. We'll discuss these in the next section. Here, it is vital to point out that humility is a virtue we are to exemplify in all our relationships and toward all people. This includes not only our neighbors, fellow citizens, and fellow Christians but all human beings, as we are able to do so. Nothing in Scripture or in the example set for us by Christ tells us that humility is limited in its scope. Christians, as citizens of the kingdom of God that surpasses all earthly kingdoms, are to exemplify humility to every single citizen of those earthly kingdoms, as we have the opportunity to do so. Humility is not optional for followers of Jesus. It is an essential part of following the way.

Another problem is that there is a deep tension, if not an outright contradiction, in the position held by many Christian nationalists. In the above passage from Torba and Isker, they say we should care for our fellow citizens, especially our siblings in Christ. But we are also supposed to place the interests of our neighbor "above the interests of foreigners in foreign nations."[7] Yet this ignores the fact that so many citizens of other lands are also our fellow brothers and sisters in Christ. Many Christian nationalists neglect this important truth. I agree that we have some special obligations to our fellow Christians, and we'll consider this in more detail below. But these special obligations are not just directed to fellow Christians who are members of our home, church, community, or nation. The church is a worldwide entity, which means that we have special obligations that extend beyond the borders of our nation, because the church extends beyond the borders of our nation. We owe much to all our fellow Christians, regardless of where they live.

Moreover, the people of other nations, regardless of their faith, are human beings made in the image of God. This is sufficient for acting in humility toward them, the type of humility Jesus demonstrated in his incarnation and crucifixion. This humility was motivated in part by his desire to draw all people to himself (John 12:32; see also 2 Pet. 3:9). As ambassadors for Christ, we must exhibit this same kind of humility toward all people.

When we are given the opportunity, there are times when we should put the interests of people from other nations ahead of the interests of those in our home, community, and nation. This doesn't mean we ignore providing for our own, or neglect their needs and interests. That's a false dilemma. We can follow the guidance of 1 Timothy 5:8 about providing for the members of our own household, *and* we can help provide for others in our community, nation, and world. Many of us don't have to choose between providing for members of our household or helping citizens of other nations, immigrants, and the undocumented. It is a both-and situation, not an either-or one. Christian morality tells us to do both, as we are able. Luke 12:48 records Jesus's teaching that "From everyone to whom much is given, much will be required, and from the one to whom much has been entrusted, even more will be demanded." Those of us in America who have the resources to do so ought to care for our families, neighbors, and communities as well as help those who don't fall within any of these groups. Humility requires that we do so. We need such humility. And from the foundation of Christlike humility, we are then able to extend Christlike love.

Love

When asked which commandment of the law was the greatest, Jesus answered, "'You shall love the Lord your God with all your heart and with all your soul and with all your mind.' This is the greatest and first commandment. And a second is like it: 'You shall love your neighbor as yourself'" (Matt. 22:37–39). We are to love God with all our being, and love our neighbor as ourself. We are to seek their good, their flourishing, their well-being, in sacrificial ways if need be. These are the highest principles of Christian ethics. This is the Great Commandment: Love God, and love your neighbor as yourself.

But love is not only a command to be obeyed, or a principle to be followed. It is also a virtue to be lived. Love is, in fact, the greatest Christian virtue. Love of another person means to will their good. The virtue of love, then, is the disposition to will the good of others.[8] One who has the virtue of love will habitually do good to and for others. With this in mind, we can see why 1 Corinthians 13 concludes, "And now faith, hope, and love remain, these three, and the greatest of these is love" (v. 13).

Love, then, is the primary component of the Great Commandment. It is also the substance of the great virtue. In love, we serve others and do what we can to satisfy their interests, to meet their needs, to contribute to their well-being. Christian nationalism, however, employs an idea of love that is not worthy of the term because it limits the scope of love in ways that Jesus himself rejected.

In Luke's gospel, the giving of the Great Commandment is followed by the parable of the Good Samaritan (Luke 10:25–37). There, an expert in the law asks what to do to inherit eternal life, and Jesus gives his answer—love God with all you are, and your neighbor as yourself. But here, because the expert in the law wanted to vindicate himself, he asks the question, "And who is my neighbor?" Jesus proceeds with the parable, in which a priest and a Levite ignore the suffering of a man robbed and severely beaten at the side of the road. A Samaritan, of all people, is the hero of the parable, the example to follow.

In the parable, the Samaritan doesn't choose to encounter this victim, but once he encounters him, he takes care of him, motivated by compassion. The Samaritan meets the immediate needs of the victim, giving him care by bandaging and treating his wounds. But he doesn't stop there. He next takes him to an inn and cares for him. Then the following day he pays the innkeeper to care for him, and he promises to pay whatever costs were incurred when he returns.

Jesus turns the question "Who is my neighbor?" on its head. Rather than saying what the expert in the law may have hoped, telling him to focus only on a specific religious or ethnic group, or even simply saying outright that everyone is your neighbor, Jesus takes a different tack. He says the question is not "Who is my neighbor?" but rather "How can I be a neighbor?" And when we ask this question, we realize that we are to be a neighbor to others as we have the opportunity to do so, to meet the needs they have as we are equipped to do so. This is how we, in the words of Jesus, "go and do likewise" (v. 37).

We've already seen Christian nationalists state that "Christian Nationalism is loving your neighbor," then follow that up with the very question the expert in the law posed to Jesus, "Who is our neighbor?"[9] The answer for Christian nationalists is often limited to their fellow citizens and fellow Christians in their own country. But this is wrong. A retelling of the parable in Christian nationalist terms will help us see why:

> A Christian nationalist asked Jesus "Who is my neighbor?" In response, Jesus told him a parable. A man was traveling on a country road when he was stopped and carjacked by a group of thieves. They took him out of his car, beat him, stripped him, stole all he had, and then drove off in his car, leaving him to die on the side of the road. He had no money, no ID, no credit cards, and nothing to eat or drink. By chance, the pastor of a large church in a nearby town was driving by, but when he saw the man, he kept driving. Then a deeply patriotic American came to the scene of the crime, but seeing the man bloodied and beaten on the side of the road, he also kept driving. Finally, an undocumented immigrant drove by. Seeing this man beaten, mostly naked, and in danger of dying, he stopped and helped him. He put antibiotic ointment on his wounds and bandaged them. He put the man in the back seat of his car and took him to a local hospital. He stayed there until he was sure the man was okay and would be cared for by the hospital staff. He even told the staff that if the man didn't have any money, he would help pay for his care if needed. When the Christian nationalist was asked "Who was a neighbor to this robbery victim?" he could not bring himself to say "The undocumented immigrant," and instead simply said "The one who showed mercy to him." Jesus then said, "Go and do likewise."

The question "Who is my neighbor?" reveals a misunderstanding of the heart of Christ and how citizens of God's kingdom are to act in the world. It reveals a misunderstanding of what it is to love God with heart, soul, mind, and strength, and what it means to love our neighbor as ourselves. The question tries to limit the scope of the obligation to love our neighbor, but Jesus will have none of that. The scope is not limited, at least not in the way we might want. We don't *ask* who our neighbor is—we seek to *be* a neighbor to all whom God brings across our path, to all he gives us the ability to care for and serve. Often this will be our physical neighbors, but this is not a requirement. The Samaritan was not a physical neighbor of the robbery victim, but he chose to be a neighbor to him, tending to his wounds and making sure he was cared for as he recovered. But Christian nationalists often want to limit the scope of such love to people in our homes and communities, our fellow citizens. They want to limit the scope of the obligation to love our neighbor, but Jesus will have none of that.

There are no religious, racial, ethnic, socioeconomic, or national boundaries that restrict the Great Commandment. There is something important, however, about our commitment to our local community, and the local body of Christ of which we are members. We should not ignore this. Paul is helpful when he instructs the Galatians, "Whenever we have an opportunity, let us work for the good of all and especially for those of the family of faith" (6:10). It is true that charity begins at home, in this sense, but for Christians it doesn't end there.[10] We are to love not only our fellow believers and fellow citizens but all people, including our enemies. We do have special obligations to our fellow Christians, in virtue of the relationship we have with them. In the context of Galatians, the point is that we are to help them when they are struggling with sin by gently restoring them. We are to bear their burdens, and they ours (6:1-2). We must share with those who teach us the word (6:6). The point is not that we should value other Christians more highly than everyone else, but rather that we do good to anyone we have the opportunity to help, and that we have particular obligations to those in our local family of faith by nature of our shared faith in Christ, as just described. The nature of the help Paul has in mind is using our resources, including money, to help people in the church and the wider community. There is a specific moral and financial responsibility to others in the church, to be sure, yet "from the start Jesus's followers understood their mission, precisely as part of bringing the good news of God's kingdom into real life, as being 'to do good to everyone.'"[11] If we seek to limit "the only thing that counts," which is "faith working through love" (Gal. 5:6), solely to those in our home, our church, our local community, or our fellow citizens, we violate the letter and spirit of the law of Christ.

Let's consider a specific application that American Christian nationalists attempt to make, having to do with an analogy between the love of one's family and the love of one's nation. We saw in chapter 1 that Christian nationalists claim we should prioritize our nation's interests over the interests of other nations. A nation is similar to a family, they say. Just as we prioritize the needs and interests of members of our own family over those of other people, we should prioritize the needs and interests of our nation over those of other nations. A good parent wouldn't allow their child to go hungry or not get medical care that she needs in order to provide food or medical care to another child in the community. Similarly, a nation should prefer its own interests and needs over the needs and interests of other nations.

The idea that we have stronger obligations to members of our own family is correct. We may have stronger obligations to other citizens of our nation. A government has stronger obligations to its people, and to the nation, compared to other people and their nations. The role of government is in part to secure the interests and welfare of its own people. For many Christian nationalists, this is just an extension of family-first and nation-first reasoning. The problem is that it does not hold in all cases, in the case of the family or the nation. There are exceptions, because there are other morally relevant considerations apart from family and nation that can come into play. Wolfe, for example, claims that "no individual, family, or nation is duty-bound to welcome strangers to the detriment of the good of those most near and bound [to] it."[12] This is false. Let's consider why.

Consider the family. While it is true that, all else being equal, I have stronger obligations to my children than to the children of others, there are exceptions to this. It's true that if I face a choice between feeding my own child and feeding the child of someone else, my first responsibility is to my own child. But there are all sorts of cases in which the prioritization of my own child does not hold, in which I can meet the basic needs of a stranger by forfeiting some luxury goods for a member of my family, or myself. For example, if I'm faced with a choice between buying my child a very expensive gift she doesn't need and feeding someone else's child, there will be plenty of cases in which I should use that money to feed the other child. The needs in play in any situation matter, not just the relationships that exist. We should not *always* put our children or our family first. There are plenty of cases in which this is the right thing to do. But there are plenty of cases in which it is not.

Similar reasoning applies to nations. It might be in our national interest to get access to cheap coltan, a metal ore used in mobile phones and other electronic devices. But this is not in the interests of people from some nations, where child labor and slave labor are used to engage in the often-dangerous mining of this metal. The price of coltan, and therefore of our devices, is lower because of this. But the cost is the violation of the basic rights of other human beings, including children. It doesn't matter that these laborers aren't fellow citizens; it is enough that they are fellow human beings. Or consider the undocumented immigrant who is a stranger to us. If we can sacrifice smaller goods, or luxury goods, in order to provide food, shelter, and physical safety for such persons, then we have a duty to do just that. We should not *always* put our nation or our fellow citizens first. There are plenty of cases in which this is the right thing to do. But there are plenty of cases in which it is not.

Love and unity are vital to Christian life and witness. Jesus tells his disciples, "By this everyone will know that you are my disciples, if you have love for one another" (John 13:35). We are to love each other with the love Christ has given us. Jesus also prays for all his followers, "As you, Father, are in me and I am in you, may they also be in us, so that the world may believe that you have sent me. The glory that you have given me I have given them, so that they may be one, as we are one" (John 17:21-22). The love of Jesus is a radical, humble, self-giving love. We are to exhibit such love. The unity that he prays his followers would exhibit is deep, reflecting the depths of the unity between the members of the Trinity.

This is another place where some nationalists' misguided and immoral views related to ethnicity rear their ugly heads. Wolfe claims, "People of different ethnic groups can exercise respect for difference, conduct some routine business with each other, join in interethnic alliances for mutual good, and exercise common humanity (e.g., the good Samaritan), but they cannot have a life together that goes beyond mutual alliance."[13] This is simply false. The deepest human relationships can and do extend across ethnic boundaries: marriage, parenting, friendship, and Christian fellowship. Wolfe has in mind civil arrangements, but the church exists within such arrangements. The idea that human beings of different ethnicities cannot have a life together beyond mere mutual alliance is problematic enough. But the idea that followers of Jesus cannot have a life together that extends beyond mere mutual alliance is clearly false, and contradicted by the vision of the church we see in the New Testament. The church is a worldwide organic unity of all people across not only ethnic boundaries but racial, cultural, and political ones too. The deepest forms of life together at all levels— personal, public, and political—can and do cross ethnic boundaries. What else could Paul mean in Galatians 3:28 when he says that "there is no longer Jew or Greek; there is no longer slave or free; there is no longer male and female, for all of you are one in Christ Jesus"? Believers are baptized into Christ, have clothed themselves with Christ, and are heirs of Christ, united together in him as the offspring of Abraham, regardless of their ethnicities. Life together in Christ is not merely a mutual alliance; it is a deep unity of soul that knows no ethnic boundary. The love of Christ and the unity of his church admit of no such division.

Christian nationalism violates the Great Commandment and the great virtue. In answer to the question "Who is my neighbor?" Christian nationalism points to those in our homes, communities, and even nation. Yet the point of the parable of the Good Samaritan is to be a neighbor, and the point of the Great Commandment is to love all those whom we have the opportunity to love. While hard decisions have to be made, we accept too much of things as they are. In a nation with our wealth and vast resources, we can do so much more to help those running from oppression, grinding poverty, violence, rape, war, and forced conscription. Certainly, there must be standards and there will be limits to what we can do, but we are nowhere near those limits, given all the resources we possess. Christian nationalism teaches us to turn inward, isolating ourselves from many people in this world. But Jesus offers us a different example, of turning toward others in humility and love, helping to alleviate their suffering and addressing the injustice in the world. This is a hard and challenging teaching. But it is a teaching of Jesus. Followers of his way must try to apply it to our lives. There is more to do for American Christians who have the means. Much more, if we want to put the words of Jesus into practice: "Go and do likewise" (Luke 10:37).

5

Christians and the Beloved Community

Where do we go from here? Should Christians engage in politics at all? If so, what should the goal of that engagement be? What does it look like to engage in politics and public life in the United States in ways that are honoring to Jesus? These are not easy questions, but they are important ones to consider. I have deep respect for those Christian traditions that limit their engagement in the political realm of life, some even entirely foregoing it. I don't enjoy reading or talking about politics in the United States, though I used to. Yet for my part, I cannot escape the conviction that many Christians should participate in politics and in political dialogue, trying to bring healing, hope, and other good things to our nation and world. Because there is still so much injustice, so much suffering, so much that is not the way it ought to be, there is important work to do for all of us, including followers of Christ. But how should Christians do that work, which Christian values are relevant, and to what end?

While some prefer keeping religious people, or at least religious arguments, out of politics, I think this is a mistake. But as I've made clear, religious people shouldn't try to keep nonreligious people, or people from other religions, out of politics. In a pluralistic society that is also a democratic republic, everyone should have the opportunity to participate and to offer arguments in support of their views. If we don't agree with someone else, we should try to show what's wrong with their view or political position, rather than trying to silence them with vitriol or insults or power.

What we need is an open and inclusive approach to politics and public life. Christians who engage in these realms should do so from a posture of love, humility, and service, rather than one of coercion, pride, and lust for power. The great principles of our nation—freedom of speech, freedom of conscience, and freedom of religion—demand such an open and inclusive approach.

In this chapter I'll focus on two questions: (i) How can we engage in politics and public life in the United States in ways that are honoring to Jesus?; and (ii) What should the goal of that engagement be? The answers to these questions are found in an ideal that was central to the thought and work of Martin Luther King Jr.—the Beloved Community.

The Beloved Community

The vision of the Beloved Community is the centerpiece of the life and work of Martin Luther King Jr.[1] It is a compelling vision for all humanity, and one that Christians have good reason to pursue. For King, the Beloved Community is the ideal form of social and political life, grounded in the Christian faith. In a particular sense, it is the ideal Christian society. As we will see, it is a society grounded in Christian ideals, but it is not a society that is *for* Christians or ruled *by* Christians. The Beloved Community is a society for *all*, where love and justice prevail. It is a society where all can flourish—Christians, Jews, Muslims, Buddhists, Hindus, people from any religious tradition or no religion at all—because the basic human dignity of all is not only respected, it is cherished.

While I agree with King that the Beloved Community is the ideal Christian society, describing it this way can be misleading.

It would be more accurate, or at least less confusing, to call the Beloved Community the ideal human society. Any religion or worldview that values humanity, works to foster the common good and the flourishing of all, has good reasons to work toward the creation of this community. The Beloved Community includes the kind of Christian values that are suitable for a nation, one that allows everyone the opportunity to flourish, without coercing people to be Christians or marginalizing anyone, regardless of their faith or lack of it. The Beloved Community, then, is the ideal *human* society.

The vision of the Beloved Community is one that is drastically different from the kind of society envisioned by Christian nationalists. It is a vision of society where there is a deep unity in all dimensions of human life. There are no racial divisions, no social or class divisions, no economic divisions, no divisions based on gender, age, or education—no divisions of any kind. Love and acceptance of others would be more than platitudes; they would be part and parcel of daily life. In the Beloved Community, we reject the psychological and emotional barriers that separate us. We overcome them. We accept and relish our interrelatedness and our interdependence. As King puts it, "The agony of the poor impoverishes the rich; the betterment of the poor enriches the rich. We are inevitably our brother's keeper because we are our brother's brother. Whatever affects one directly affects all indirectly."[2] We don't deny these truths—we embrace them. We struggle to end the injustices that are barriers to this community. Rather than building physical or metaphorical walls, and focusing solely on the good of the people in our homes, our neighborhood, and our nation, we take responsibility for one another. We do so not only because we care about justice; we do so because it is a demand of love.

In this community, we recognize our interdependence and foster solidarity. Such solidarity refuses to accept injustice. In an article honoring W. E. B. Du Bois, King praises him for his refusal to do so and exhorts us to follow his example:

Let us be dissatisfied until every man can have food and material necessities for his body, culture and education for his soul, freedom and human dignity for his spirit. Let us be dissatisfied until rat-infested, vermin-filled slums will be a thing of the dark past and every family will have a decent sanitary house in which to live. Let us be dissatisfied until the empty stomachs of Mississippi are filled and the idle industries of Appalachia are revitalized. Let us be dissatisfied until brotherhood is no longer a meaningless word at the end of a prayer but the first order of business on every legislative agenda. Let us be dissatisfied until our brother of the Third World—Asia, Africa, and Latin America—will no longer be the victim of imperialist exploitation, but will be lifted up from the long night of poverty, illiteracy, and disease, . . . until "justice will roll down like waters from a mighty stream" [Amos 5:24].[3]

This is the deep solidarity envisioned by the Beloved Community. Justice, including economic justice, is important for human flourishing. A healthy and just community will have no economic exploitation, nor will people lack for their basic material needs. In such a community, God's will that all people have both the physical and spiritual necessities of life is realized. The basic needs of all are met. There is racial equality and justice. No human being is left behind or pushed aside. In the Beloved Community, what we have and what we can do, our possessions and our talents, are put to use in service of humanity. There are respect, dignity, freedom, and justice for all. The Beloved Community includes all people: people of every race, ethnicity, class, nationality, and religion. This is the justice envisioned by King. It is also the justice envisioned by the kingdom of God and the hope proclaimed by the gospel (Luke 4:14–21).

The Beloved Community is the realization of our best ideals as Americans, including life, liberty, and the pursuit of happiness, which for King means that all people should have "three meals a day for their bodies, education and culture for their minds, and dignity, equality and freedom for their spirits."[4] For King, the Beloved Community is also grounded in the hope of the kingdom of God. In that kingdom, there is true social justice and agape love among human beings who are all full bearers of God's image. We have one Creator, and hence we are all brothers and sisters, regardless of any other difference. Because we are God's offspring, we can have unity and even community. We can have shalom: reconciliation between all human beings, in which the barriers that separate us are destroyed; freedom, including freedom to serve; and hope that God will actually renew and redeem this world, that his will can be done on earth as it is in heaven.

There is not only room for people of various religions in the Beloved Community but there is also room for people of no religion. While many Christian nationalists would reject the idea, there are important ways that atheists can be members of and equally contribute to the Beloved Community. Not only that, there are also important ways that atheists can be allied with God.

To see why, consider the following from Christian philosopher Robert Adams:

> I do *not* mean to imply that only theists should be regarded (by theists) as allied with God. . . . I am as interested here in implicit as in explicit love for God; and whether we share God's loves depends much more on what we love (for its own sake) than on whether we conceptualize it theologically. . . . In a theistic perspective, nontheists and theists are equally creatures of God, and their good impulses come equally from God. . . . So we can think of a sort of implicit alliance with God as helping to constitute an implicit love for God. Doubtless alliance with God can be more fully developed if it is theologically explicit, but such theological explicitness does not guarantee the authenticity of such alliance.[5]

Adams is right. A Christian might have an explicit love for God, expressed in their daily life and worship. But all human beings, as bearers of God's image, have good impulses that come from God. An atheist who works for human equality, or who spends time serving the poor, or who is passionate about the human rights of all, is allied with God and expresses an implicit love for God and the things God loves in these ways. Certainly, from a Christian point of view it is better to develop this implicit love of God into an explicit love grounded in faith in God. But many are tempted to think that theological explicitness, that is, saying we believe "the right" Christian things, is all that matters, or is what matters most.

But if Adams is right, an atheist can be more allied with God than the theist who may express in clear and direct terms her own allegiance to God. What matters in this context, as Adams points out, is what we value for its own sake. I would add that how this plays out in our actions is crucial as well.

All who possess and show compassion are allied with God. The atheist who values the welfare of other human beings for its own sake is more aligned with God than the theist who values the accumulation of power and wealth over her family, friends, and other people. The atheist who values the beauty of the natural world is more aligned with the teachings of Christ than the Christian who is devoted to conspicuous consumption. The atheist who works to meet the needs of undocumented immigrants fleeing injustice, poverty, persecution, and violence is more aligned with Jesus than the Christian who supports placing a string of buoys with rotating saw blades on the Rio Grande, like a scene out of *The Hunger Games* movies.

To be sure, there are deep disagreements on important moral and political issues in our time, but if we think of each other as allies of the good whenever possible, rather than as enemies, perhaps we can carve out enough common ground to work together for the common good. For the Christian, this can constitute an explicit love for God, as she may identify the good with God. For the atheist, such love will be implicit and therefore unrecognized as a love for God. But either way, there is common ground to be had and a common good to be pursued. And the Beloved Community provides the space for all of us to do just that.

Christian nationalists, however, reject such common ground and reject the goals and substance of the Beloved Community. Wolfe, for example, argues that our love for others is more intense the more similar they are to us, and that this is not a result of sin. It is a part of our human nature, as God intended it to be.[6] Contrast this with King's 1967 Christmas sermon on peace, in which he proclaims that if we really want peace on this planet, "our loyalties must transcend our race, our tribe, our class, and our nation."[7] But it's not just King who affirms this truth. This preference for being with people like oneself—members of one's own culture, race, or ethnic group—is not how God intended it to be. We know this for many reasons, but one is that at the end of all things, when the new heavens and new earth are finally brought into being, we will serve and praise and enjoy God together, alongside people from every tribe, tongue, and nation (Rev. 7:9). This is where God is leading us; this is the next step in the story of humanity. We won't oppose it then, and we should not oppose it now.

Adam Russell Taylor develops and applies King's vision to our day. One value of the Beloved Community is what Taylor calls "radical welcome."[8] Radical welcome can be seen throughout the Bible in the consistent refrain from God to Israel to welcome the stranger, and in the teachings of Jesus to care for the least of these (Matt. 25:40–45). When applied to our contemporary immigration situation, a crisis that is in part the result of decades of Congress's failure to act, radical welcome compels the follower of Christ to treat all who come to our country, including those who do so illegally, humanely because they bear God's image. Politicians and pundits stoke fear through lies for the sake of power or profit. A large number of undocumented persons came here legally but have overstayed the limit on their visas.[9] Native-born Americans commit crime at higher rates than undocumented immigrants.[10] Immigrants actually contribute to American prosperity.[11] It will take courage, moral imagination, and a commitment to our best and deepest values, but we can once again be a people known for welcoming the immigrant, the oppressed, the persecuted, and the poor. We are resource rich and compassion poor. But we can change that. And we must, if we want to see the Beloved Community come to be.

This is one of the starkest differences between the Beloved Community and Christian nationalist visions of America. The Beloved Community is a community for all. It reflects the best ideals of America. More importantly for followers of Jesus, it is faithful to central Christian values. There will be limits to what we can do as a nation, but Christians are not limited by national borders. The body of Christ can work in every nation to bring about this community, realizing the hope of the gospel throughout the world.

The means to bringing about the Beloved Community contrasts sharply with the acceptance and even propagation of violence we see in the rhetoric of many Christian nationalists. King emphasized the importance of nonviolence as the path to this ideal. Nonviolence is the only appropriate means because one cannot form a community with love, trust, and understanding—values that bind the Beloved Community together—on the foundation of violence. The goal determines the means that are appropriate for achieving it. Since the Beloved Community is the goal, nonviolence is the means. No other method or strategy for action is appropriate. This doesn't mean those who are working to bring about this community are passive. If other methods don't work, a strategy including nonviolent mass civil disobedience is a live option. But violence is off the table.

To make progress toward the formation of the Beloved Community, leaders must take responsibility for the influence they wield, using it wisely and well. There is good evidence that both faith leaders and policymakers can have a significant influence on

Christians who believe, or may be more disposed to believe, some or all the elements of Christian nationalism.[12] While I understand the reticence of pastors in particular to address Christian nationalism, we simply cannot ignore it. In many ways, a pastoral focus on the Scriptures, on keeping in step with the Spirit, and on helping church members have hearts and minds that are shaped by Christ in community is the best way to resist Christian nationalism. But if pastors and other leaders address its problems, especially the ways Christian nationalism contradicts "the faith that was once and for all handed on to the saints" (Jude 3), there is good evidence that it will make a significant difference.

Another essential requirement, if we are to move toward the realization of the Beloved Community, is repentance. Only then can we experience greater reconciliation and restoration in our relationships with God and one another. There is much to be repented of in our country. Our devotion to material wealth rather than dedication to the marginalized. Our prioritizing of our purported national interests above the needs of immigrants. Our dependence on military might for security, rather than a deepening commitment to the welfare of all nations. Our dehumanizing and degrading treatment of Indigenous peoples and other minorities, rather than endeavors to secure liberty and justice for all. These are high ideals, but they are worth the effort. And the starting point for making further progress is repentance. Repentance is not weakness; it is not to be rejected as "woke." It is actually the key to reconciliation, which is essential for any flourishing human community made up of fallen human beings, including the Beloved Community.

The Beloved Community is for all of us, simply because we are human and bear God's image. Any person of sound mind and good heart would want to live in such a community, because the basic rights, needs, and interests of all are taken seriously. We take responsibility for each other. No one is excluded, and no one is given pride of place. All stand on the same level ground. It is not being human and being Christian, being human and being American, being human and being white, being human and being male, being human and being heterosexual. All are welcome in this community. Being human is enough. All are valued. All are loved.

Some, including King, have enough faith in humanity's potential for goodness and the power of love that they think the Beloved Community can become a reality in this life. The process may be slow, but with God's help they believe it can happen. Others are skeptical and think it will come about only in the next. While it may be true that this community will be completely realized only in the next life, we can get a lot closer to it in this life than we are at present. This is down to not only our potential for goodness and the power of love but the power of God as we work in partnership with God, for God's kingdom to come, for God's will to be done, on earth as it is in heaven, where a Beloved Community beyond all that we can imagine at present will finally, and fully, exist.

Our True Home

We've taken a hard look at problems for Christian nationalism, from both an American and a Christian perspective. As I've thought about what lies beneath contemporary Christian nationalism, a few things come to mind.

Part of the problem with how many American Christians think about politics, and participate in them, has to do with our unique history. Our founders used religious language in our founding documents and in many of their other writings. Religion is a central part of the American story, for better and for worse.

Some American Christians have been aligned with the government for a long time, in many ways, and therefore they have failed in many ways to call it to account. Many have been comfortable with their relationship to the government and are used to their interests aligning with the interests and power of the state. When they feel this slipping away, the impulse to grasp onto privilege and power can be quite strong.

There is a blind spot among white American Christians, in particular, about the past. Many of them tend to idealize the 1950s as a golden age that America should get back to, "taking our country back" to the good old days. But the good old days weren't good for everyone. The massacres of Native Americans and the theft of their lands, slavery, Jim Crow, segregation, and continued racism, sexism, and exploitation of children are also key parts of the American story before, during, and after the '50s.

In a 2022 interview, Voddie Baucham, author and dean of the School of Divinity at African Christian University in Zambia, said, "If you don't want Christian nationalism, what other kind of nationalism do you want? Do you want . . . secular nationalism, Muslim nationalism . . . or if it's not the Christianity that's the problem, is it the nationalism that's the problem? If you don't want nationalism, what do you want? Do you want globalism? No thank you."[13] We shouldn't want *any* kind of nationalism in which the interests of some are prioritized over the interests of others. We should want a nation and a world that reflect love, peace, and justice for all. We should want a patriotism that focuses on our good, the common good, and is willing to sacrifice for that good in both the national and international realms. Many American Christians simply assume that they have a right to a society that reflects their version of Christian morality, coercing others to fall in line. This is, to put it bluntly, false. We have no such right. We do have the right to offer arguments, using reason to persuade others that our view is correct. We do have the right to live authentic lives of faith, and to pray for our communities, our nation, and our world. We do have the right to love and serve in all domains of society, including politics. But we don't have a right to some vision of a Christian nation that excludes our supposed enemies and protects our power and privilege.

I suspect that the longing for a Christian America is a distortion of a good longing, a longing for our true home. Torba and Isker are mistaken when, in the context of the culture war, they say that "for American Christians to fight back against these things, we have to be willing to say 'not only is this world indeed our home, this world belongs to Jesus Christ.'"[14] The biblical authors knew that this world is indeed *not* our home. We are "aliens and exiles" in this world (2 Pet. 2:11). We are not citizens of this world, but rather "our citizenship is in heaven" (Phil. 3:20). The heroes of the faith in Hebrews 11 "confessed that they were strangers and foreigners on the earth" (v. 13); they desired "a better homeland, that is, a heavenly one" (v. 16). We, like all who follow Christ, must come to know in our bones that "here we have no lasting city, but we are looking for the city that is to come" (Heb. 13:14). There is great beauty and goodness in our world. But it is not our home. What is true, good, and beautiful about the Beloved Community is that it mimics what life will be like in our true home. But it does not mistake this world as our true home, at least not in its present state.

The U2 song "Invisible" includes the refrain "There is no them; there's only us." This expresses a central part of the vision of the Beloved Community. This is what we must strive for in our words and deeds, providing a human example of deep unity, community, humility, justice, and love. Let's try to create a world, or at least try to move closer to a world, where it is simply *us*, not us *versus* them or even us *and* them. Only us, as the song says. Let's hope, pray, and work for such a world, as we anticipate another world where our true home awaits.

Notes

Chapter 1

1. Candy Woodall, "Marjorie Taylor Greene Compares Trump to Jesus before His Arrest and Arraignment in New York," *USA Today*, April 4, 2023, https://www.usatoday.com/story/news/politics/2023/04/04/marjorie-taylor-greene-trump-jesus-arrest/11600165002/.

2. Gene Healy, *The Cult of the Presidency, Updated: America's Dangerous Devotion to Executive Power* (Washington, DC: Cato Institute, 2009), 283.

3. Robert P. Jones, "The Roots of Christian Nationalism Go Back Further Than You Think," *Time*, August 31, 2023, https://time.com/6309657/us-christian-nationalism-columbus-essay/.

4. Lisa Sharon Harper, *Fortune: How Race Broke My Family and the World—and How to Repair It All* (Grand Rapids: Brazos Press, 2022), 90.

5. "Bono Speech at Georgetown—Keeping Faith with the Idea of America," video, 1:39, June 24, 2014, https://www.youtube.com/watch?v=Tg3Xzh2cXD8.

6. Ashley Lopez, "More Than Half of Republicans Support Christian Nationalism, according to a New Survey," All Things Considered, *NPR*, February 14, 2023, https://www.npr.org/2023/02/14/1156642544/more-than-half-of-republicans-support-christian-nationalism-according-to-a-new-s.

7. Conrad Swanson, "Lauren Boebert Told Congregation She's 'Tired of This Separation of Church and State Junk,'" *Denver Post*, June 27, 2022, https://www.denverpost.com/2022/06/27/lauren-boebert-church-state-colorado/.

8. Public Religion Research Institute (PRRI) Staff, "A Christian Nation? Understanding the Threat of Christian Nationalism to American Democracy and Culture," *PRRI* (blog), February 8, 2023, https://www.prri.org/research/a-christian-nation-understanding-the-threat-of-christian-nationalism-to-american-democracy-and-culture/.

9. Yoram Hazony, *The Virtue of Nationalism* (New York: Basic Books, 2018), 3.

10. Paul D. Miller, *The Religion of American Greatness: What's Wrong with Christian Nationalism* (Downers Grove, IL: IVP Academic, 2022), 30.

11. Andrew Torba and Andrew Isker, *Christian Nationalism: A Biblical Guide for Taking Dominion and Discipling Nations* (n.p.: Gab AI, 2022), 72.

12. See John Fea, *Was America Founded as a Christian Nation? A Historical Introduction* (Louisville: Westminster John Knox, 2016); and Thomas S. Kidd, *America's Religious History: Faith, Politics, and the Shaping of a Nation* (Grand Rapids: Zondervan Academic, 2019).

13. Miller, *Religion of American Greatness*, 31, 59.

14. Samuel P. Huntington, *Who Are We: The Challenges to America's National Identity* (New York: Simon & Schuster, 2004), xvi.

15. Stephen Wolfe, *The Case for Christian Nationalism* (Moscow, ID: Canon, 2022), 9–15.

16. Leonardo Blair, "Missionary Sean Feucht Insists That Christians Should Rule Nation and Write Laws," *Christian Post*, April 26, 2023, https://www.christianpost.com/news/missionary-sean-feucht-insists-that-christians-should-rule-nation.html.

17. Wolfe, *Case for Christian Nationalism*, 322.

18. Torba and Isker, *Christian Nationalism*, 70.

19. "Inaugural Address," *The American Presidency Project*, January 20, 2017, https://www.presidency.ucsb.edu/documents/inaugural-address-14.

20. Tobias Cremer, *The Godless Crusade* (New York: Cambridge University Press, 2023), 11.

21. Torba and Isker, *Christian Nationalism*, 30.

22. Katherine Stewart, *The Power Worshippers: Inside the Dangerous Rise of Religious Nationalism* (New York: Bloomsbury, 2020), 3.

Chapter 2

1. George Orwell, "Notes on Nationalism," *Polemic* (1945), https://www.orwellfoundation.com/the-orwell-foundation/orwell/essays-and-other-works/notes-on-nationalism/.

2. For understanding these values, I rely on the work of Tom Morris in his *The Everyday Patriot: How to Be a Great American Now* (Wisdom/Work, 2022), 70–83.

3. Miller, *Religion of American Greatness*, 75.

4. Andrew L. Whitehead and Samuel L. Perry, *Taking America Back for God: Christian Nationalism in the United States* (New York: Oxford University Press, 2020), 161.

5. Torba and Isker, *Christian Nationalism*, 46.

6. US Const. art. VI.

7. US Const. amend. I.

8. Torba and Isker, *Christian Nationalism*, 72, 78.

9. Wolfe, *Case for Christian Nationalism*, 358, 391.

10. Morris, *Everyday Patriot*, 76.

11. Wolfe, *Case for Christian Nationalism*, 346.

12. Blair, "Christians Should Rule Nation."

13. Torba and Isker, *Christian Nationalism*, 10.

14. Torba and Isker, *Christian Nationalism*, 46.

15. Torba and Isker, *Christian Nationalism*, 25.

16. Andrew Torba (@BasedTorba), Twitter (X) August 16, 2023, https://web.archive.org/web/20230818161157/https://twitter.com/BasedTorba/status/1691824378277687587.

17. "Andrew Torba: Five Things to Know," Anti-Defamation League, August 19, 2022, updated November 28, 2022, https://www.adl.org/resources/blog/andrew-torba-five-things-know-0.

18. Stephen Wolfe (@PerfInjust), Twitter (X), April 17, 2023, https://twitter.com/PerfInjust/status/1647931701773860865.

19. Stephen Wolfe (@PerfInjust), Twitter (X), July 28, 2021, https://twitter.com/PerfInjust/status/1420385874492203015. Wolfe writes "bl*ack men" in the tweet; I've edited for clarity. The tweet has since been at least partially deleted but can be found in full at https://onpeacefulnoncompliance.substack.com/p/stephen-wolfe-and-1352 #footnote-14-106406080.

20. Allen J. Beck, *Race and Ethnicity of Violent Crime Offenders and Arrestees, 2018*, Bureau of Justice Statistics (Washington, DC: US Department of Justice, 2021).

21. Stephen Wolfe, "Anarcho-Tyranny in 2022," *IM—1776* (blog), March 18, 2022, https://im1776.com/2022/03/18/anarcho-tyranny/.

22. Blake Callens, draft of *The Case against Christian Nationalism: A Commentary on Stephen Wolfe's Book*, 100.

23. Wolfe, *Case for Christian Nationalism*, 453.

24. Torba and Isker, *Christian Nationalism*, 45.

25. Wolfe, *Case for Christian Nationalism*, 167.

26. Morris, *The Everyday Patriot*, 82.

27. Morris, *The Everyday Patriot*, 94–95.

Chapter 3

1. Dietrich Bonhoeffer, *Discipleship* (Minneapolis: Fortress, 2015), 114.

2. Andrew Torba and Andrew Isker, *Christian Nationalism: A Biblical Guide for Taking Dominion and Discipling Nations* (n.p.: Gab AI, 2022), 17.

3. Dietrich Bonhoeffer, "Sermon on 2 Corinthians 12:9," in *London, 1933–1935*, vol. 13. of *Dietrich Bonhoeffer Works* (Minneapolis: Fortress, 2007), 402–3.

4. Brian Kaylor and Beau Underwood, "The Sermon Michael Flynn Hopes You'll Hear," *Word & Way*, July 14, 2022, https://wordandway.org/2022/07/14/the-sermon-michael-flynn-hopes-youll-hear/.

5. Miller, *Religion of American Greatness*, 53.

6. Torba and Isker, *Christian Nationalism*, 17, 19.

7. Scott Detrow, Gabriel J. Sánchez, and Sarah Handel, "He Was a Top

Church Official Who Criticized Trump. He Says Christianity Is in Crisis," *NPR*, August 8, 2023, https://www.npr.org/2023/08/08/1192663920/southern-baptist-convention-donald-trump-christianity.

8. Torba and Isker, *Christian Nationalism*, 45, 50, 51, 52.

9. Wolfe, *Case for Christian Nationalism*, 467.

10. Wolfe, *Case for Christian Nationalism*, 469.

11. Lee C. Camp, *Scandalous Witness: A Little Political Manifesto for Christians* (Grand Rapids: Eerdmans, 2020), 37.

12. Bonhoeffer, *Discipleship*, 102–3.

13. Torba and Isker, *Christian Nationalism*, 16.

14. C. S. Lewis, *Mere Christianity* (San Francisco: HarperOne, 2015), 177.

15. Dallas Willard, *The Divine Conspiracy: Rediscovering Our Hidden Life in God*, 1st ed. (San Francisco: Harper, 1998), 283–84.

16. Dietrich Bonhoeffer, *Life Together* (Minneapolis: Fortress, 2015), 18.

17. Wolfe, *Case for Christian Nationalism*, 332.

18. Wolfe, *Case for Christian Nationalism*, 338.

19. Torba and Isker, *Christian Nationalism*, 66.

20. Torba and Isker, *Christian Nationalism*, 28.

21. Michael W. Austin, *God and Guns in America* (Grand Rapids: Eerdmans, 2020), 101–5.

22. See Torba and Isker, *Christian Nationalism*.

23. James Silberman and Dusty Deevers, *The Statement on Christian Nationalism and the Gospel* (web page), ed. by William Wolfe, Joel Webbon, Jeff Wright, and Cory Anderson, revised May 23, 2023, https://www.statementonchristiannationalism.com/.

24. Torba and Isker, *Christian Nationalism*, 29.

25. Martin Luther King Jr., "A Knock at Midnight," in *Strength to Love* (New York: Harper and Row, 1963), 47.

26. Joel B. Green, Scot McKnight, and I. Howard Marshall, eds., *Dictionary of Jesus and the Gospel* (Downers Grove, IL: IVP Academic, 1992), 680–81.

27. Craig S. Keener, *The Gospel of Matthew: A Socio-Rhetorical Commentary* (Grand Rapids: Eerdmans, 2009), 718–21.

28. PRRI Staff, "A Christian Nation?," *PRRI* (blog).

29. PRRI/Brookings Christian Nationalism Survey, 2023, quoted in PRRI Staff, "A Christian Nation?," *PRRI* (blog).

30. PRRI/Brookings Christian Nationalism Survey, 2023.

31. PRRI/Brookings Christian Nationalism Survey, 2023.

32. PRRI/Brookings Christian Nationalism Survey, 2023.

33. Janis Bowdler and Benjamin Harris, "Racial Inequality in the United States," US Department of the Treasury, July 21, 2022, https://home.treasury.gov/news/featured-stories/racial-inequality-in-the-united-states.

34. Michael W. Austin and Gregory L. Bock, eds., *QAnon, Chaos, and the Cross: Christianity and Conspiracy Theories* (Grand Rapids: Eerdmans, 2023), x–xiii.

35. Michael W. Austin, *Humility: Rediscovering the Way of Love and Life in Christ* (Grand Rapids: Eerdmans, 2024).

36. Willard, *Divine Conspiracy*, 291.

Chapter 4

1. Hazony, *Virtue of Nationalism*, 229, 231.

2. Paul K. Moser, *The Evidence for God: Religious Knowledge Reexamined* (New York: Cambridge University Press, 2009), 91.

3. Dietrich Bonhoeffer, *Letters and Papers from Prison* (Minneapolis: Fortress, 2015), 502.

4. Bonhoeffer, *Letters and Papers from Prison*, 503–4.

5. Torba and Isker, *Christian Nationalism*, 70.

6. Torba and Isker, *Christian Nationalism*, 17.

7. Torba and Isker, *Christian Nationalism*, 17.

8. Dallas Willard, *Knowing Christ Today* (New York: HarperOne, 2009), 83–93.

9. Torba and Isker, *Christian Nationalism*, 17.

10. John Stott, *The Message of Galatians* (Downers Grove, IL: IVP Academic, 1984), 136.

11. N. T. Wright, *Galatians* (Grand Rapids: Eerdmans, 2021), 495.

12. Wolfe, *Case for Christian Nationalism*, 167.

13. Wolfe, *Case for Christian Nationalism*, 147–48.

Chapter 5

1. Kenneth L. Smith and Ira G. Zepp Jr., *Search for the Beloved Community: The Thinking of Martin Luther King Jr.* (Valley Forge, PA: Judson, 1998). Most of what follows in this section is drawn from chapter 6.

2. Martin Luther King Jr., *Where Do We Go from Here: Chaos or Community?* (Boston: Beacon, 2010), 133.

3. Martin Luther King Jr., "Honoring Dr. Du Bois," *Freedomways* 8, no. 2 (1968), 110–11.

4. Martin Luther King Jr., "Nobel Prize Acceptance Speech," in *A Testament of Hope: The Essential Writings of Martin Luther King, Jr.*, ed. James Melvin Washington (San Francisco: Harper and Row, 1986), 226.

5. Robert Merrihew Adams, *Finite and Infinite Goods: A Framework for Ethics* (New York: Oxford University Press, 2002), 198.

6. Wolfe, *Case for Christian Nationalism*, 148–49.

7. Martin Luther King Jr., "A Christmas Sermon on Peace," in Washington, *A Testament of Hope*, 253.

8. Adam Russell Taylor, *A More Perfect Union: A New Vision for Building the Beloved Community* (Minneapolis: Broadleaf, 2021), 155–64.

9. Mark Hugo Lopez, Jeffrey S. Passel, and D'vera Cohn, "Key Facts about the Changing U.S. Unauthorized Immigrant Population," Pew Research Center, April 13, 2021, https://www.pewresearch.org/short -reads/2021/04/13/key-facts-about-the-changing-u-s-unauthorized -immigrant-population/.

10. Michael T. Light, Jingying He, and Jason P. Robey, "Comparing Crime Rates between Undocumented Immigrants, Legal Immigrants, and Native-Born US Citizens in Texas," *Proceedings of the National Academy of Sciences* 117, no. 51 (December 2020): 32340–47, https://www.ojp .gov/library/publications/comparing-crime-rates-between-undocu mented-immigrants-legal-immigrants-and.

11. Arloc Sherman, Danilo Trisi, Chad Stone, Shelby Gonzales, and

Sharon Parrott, "Immigrants Contribute Greatly to U.S. Economy, Despite Administration's 'Public Charge' Rule Rationale," Center on Budget and Policy Priorities, August 15, 2019, https://doi.org/10.1073/pnas.2014704117.

12. Cremer, *Godless Crusade*, 7–11.

13. @smashbaals, "Voddie Baucham on why Christian Nationalism is the only way forward," Twitter (X) (video), November 4, 2022, https://twitter.com/smashbaals/status/1588640506393014272.

14. Torba and Isker, *Christian Nationalism*, 32.

Bibliography

Adams, Robert Merrihew. *Finite and Infinite Goods: A Framework for Ethics.* New York: Oxford University Press, 2002.

Austin, Michael W. *God and Guns in America.* Grand Rapids: Eerdmans, 2020.

———. *Humility: Rediscovering the Way of Love and Life in Christ.* Grand Rapids: Eerdmans, 2024.

Austin, Michael W., and Gregory L. Bock, eds. *QAnon, Chaos, and the Cross: Christianity and Conspiracy Theories.* Grand Rapids: Eerdmans, 2023.

Beck, Allen J. *Race and Ethnicity of Violent Crime Offenders and Arrestees, 2018.* Bureau of Justice Statistics. Washington, DC: US Department of Justice, 2021.

Blair, Leonardo. "Missionary Sean Feucht Insists That Christians Should Rule Nation and Write Laws." *Christian Post,* April 26, 2023. https://www.christianpost.com/news/missionary-sean-feucht-insists-that-christians-should-rule-nation.html.

Bonhoeffer, Dietrich. *Discipleship.* Minneapolis: Fortress, 2015.

———. *Letters and Papers from Prison.* Minneapolis: Fortress, 2015.

———. *Life Together.* Minneapolis: Fortress, 2015.

———. *London, 1933–1935.* Vol. 13. of *Dietrich Bonhoeffer Works,* edited by Keith Clements. Minneapolis: Fortress, 2007.

Bowdler, Janis, and Benjamin Harris. "Racial Inequality in the United States." US Department of the Treasury. July 21, 2022. https://home.treasury.gov/news/featured-stories/racial-inequality-in-the-united-states.

Camp, Lee C. *Scandalous Witness: A Little Political Manifesto for Christians.* Grand Rapids: Eerdmans, 2020.

Cremer, Tobias. *The Godless Crusade.* New York: Cambridge University Press, 2023.

Detrow, Scott, Gabriel J. Sánchez, and Sarah Handel. "He Was a Top Church Official Who Criticized Trump. He Says Christianity Is in Crisis." *NPR*, August 8, 2023. https://www.npr.org/2023/08/08/1192663920 /southern-baptist-convention-donald-trump-christianity.

Fea, John. *Was America Founded as a Christian Nation? A Historical Introduction.* Louisville: Westminster John Knox, 2016.

Green, Joel B., Scot McKnight, and I. Howard Marshall, eds. *Dictionary of Jesus and the Gospels.* Downers Grove, IL: IVP Academic, 1992.

Harper, Lisa Sharon. *Fortune: How Race Broke My Family and the World—and How to Repair It All.* Grand Rapids: Brazos, 2022.

Hazony, Yoram. *The Virtue of Nationalism.* New York: Basic Books, 2018.

Healy, Gene. *The Cult of the Presidency, Updated: America's Dangerous Devotion to Executive Power.* Washington, DC: Cato Institute, 2009.

Huntington, Samuel P. *Who Are We: The Challenges to America's National Identity.* New York: Simon & Schuster, 2004.

Jones, Robert P. "The Roots of Christian Nationalism Go Back Further Than You Think." *Time*, August 31, 2023. https://time.com/6309657/us -christian-nationalism-columbus-essay/.

Kaylor, Brian, and Beau Underwood. "The Sermon Michael Flynn Hopes You'll Hear." *Word & Way*, July 14, 2022. https://wordandway.org/2022 /07/14/the-sermon-michael-flynn-hopes-youll-hear/.

Keener, Craig S. *The Gospel of Matthew: A Socio-Rhetorical Commentary.* Grand Rapids: Eerdmans, 2009.

Kidd, Thomas S. *America's Religious History: Faith, Politics, and the Shaping of a Nation.* Grand Rapids: Zondervan Academic, 2019.

King, Martin Luther, Jr. "A Christmas Sermon on Peace." In *A Testament of Hope: The Essential Writings of Martin Luther King, Jr.*, edited by James Melvin Washington, 253–58. San Francisco: Harper and Row, 1986.

———. "Honoring Dr. Du Bois." *Freedomways* 8, no. 2 (1968): 104–11.

———. "A Knock at Midnight." In *Strength to Love.* New York: Harper and Row, 1963.

———. "Nobel Prize Acceptance Speech." In *A Testament of Hope: The Essential Writings of Martin Luther King, Jr.*, edited by James Melvin Washington, 224–26. San Francisco: Harper and Row, 1986.

———. *Where Do We Go from Here: Chaos or Community?* Boston: Beacon, 2010.

Lewis, C. S. *Mere Christianity.* San Francisco: HarperOne, 2015.

Light, Michael T., Jingying He, and Jason P. Robey. "Comparing Crime Rates between Undocumented Immigrants, Legal Immigrants, and Native-

Born US Citizens in Texas." *Proceedings of the National Academy of Sciences* 117, no. 51 (December 2020): 32340–47. https://www.ojp.gov/li brary/publications/comparing-crime-rates-between-undocumented -immigrants-legal-immigrants-and.

Lopez, Ashley. "More Than Half of Republicans Support Christian Nationalism, according to a New Survey." All Things Considered, *NPR*, February 14, 2023. https://www.npr.org/2023/02/14/1156642544/more -than-half-of-republicans-support-christian-nationalism-according -to-a-new-s.

Lopez, Mark Hugo, Jeffrey S. Passel, and D'vera Cohn. "Key Facts about the Changing U.S. Unauthorized Immigrant Population." Pew Research Center. April 13, 2021. https://www.pewresearch.org/short -reads/2021/04/13/key-facts-about-the-changing-u-s-unauthorized -immigrant-population/.

Miller, Paul D. *The Religion of American Greatness: What's Wrong with Christian Nationalism.* Downers Grove, IL: IVP Academic, 2022.

Morris, Tom. *The Everyday Patriot: How to Be a Great American Now.* Wisdom/ Work, 2022.

Moser, Paul K. *The Evidence for God: Religious Knowledge Reexamined.* New York: Cambridge University Press, 2009.

Orwell, George. "Notes on Nationalism." *Polemic* (1945). https://www.or wellfoundation.com/the-orwell-foundation/orwell/essays-and -other-works/notes-on-nationalism/.

Public Religion Research Institute (PRRI) Staff. "A Christian Nation? Understanding the Threat of Christian Nationalism to American Democracy and Culture." *PRRI* (blog). February 8, 2023. https://www .prri.org/research/a-christian-nation-understanding-the-threat-of -christian-nationalism-to-american-democracy-and-culture/.

Sherman, Arloc, Danilo Trisi, Chad Stone, Shelby Gonzales, and Sharon Parrott. "Immigrants Contribute Greatly to U.S. Economy, Despite Administration's 'Public Charge' Rule Rationale." Center on Budget and Policy Priorities. August 15, 2019. https://doi.org/10.1073/pnas .2014704117.

Silberman, James, and Dusty Deevers. *The Statement on Christian Nationalism and the Gospel* (web page). Edited by William Wolfe, Joel Webbon, Jeff Wright, and Cory Anderson. Revised May 23, 2023. https://www .statementonchristiannationalism.com/.

Smith, Kenneth L., and Ira G. Zepp Jr. *Search for the Beloved Community: The Thinking of Martin Luther King Jr.* Valley Forge, PA: Judson, 1998.

Stewart, Katherine. *The Power Worshippers: Inside the Dangerous Rise of Religious Nationalism*. New York: Bloomsbury, 2020.

Stott, John. *The Message of Galatians*. Downers Grove, IL: IVP Academic, 1984.

Swanson, Conrad. "Lauren Boebert Told Congregation She's 'Tired of This Separation of Church and State Junk.'" *Denver Post*, June 27, 2022. https://www.denverpost.com/2022/06/27/lauren-boebert -church-state-colorado/.

Taylor, Adam Russell. *A More Perfect Union: A New Vision for Building the Beloved Community*. Minneapolis: Broadleaf, 2021.

Torba, Andrew, and Andrew Isker. *Christian Nationalism: A Biblical Guide for Taking Dominion and Discipling Nations*. N.p.: Gab AI, 2022.

Whitehead, Andrew L., and Samuel L. Perry. *Taking America Back for God: Christian Nationalism in the United States*. New York: Oxford University Press, 2020.

Willard, Dallas. *The Divine Conspiracy: Rediscovering Our Hidden Life in God*. San Francisco: Harper, 1998.

———. *Knowing Christ Today*. New York: HarperOne, 2009.

Wolfe, Stephen. "Anarcho-Tyranny in 2022." *IM—1776* (blog), March 18, 2022. https://im1776.com/2022/03/18/anarcho-tyranny/.

———. *The Case for Christian Nationalism*. Moscow, ID: Canon, 2022.

Woodall, Candy. "Marjorie Taylor Greene Compares Trump to Jesus before His Arrest and Arraignment in New York." *USA Today*, April 4, 2023. https://www.usatoday.com/story/news/politics/2023/04/04/marjo rie-taylor-greene-trump-jesus-arrest/11600165002/.

Wright, N. T. *Galatians*. Grand Rapids: Eerdmans, 2021.

Index